THE HOPE OF GLORY

By the same author

ARCHBISHOP MOWLL: *a biography*
MAKERS OF OUR HERITAGE
MASTERS OF THE ENGLISH REFORMATION
PIONEERS OF THE REFORMATION IN ENGLAND

To

THE RIGHT REVEREND

ARTHUR JOHN DAIN

Bishop-Coadjutor in the Diocese of Sydney

Close friend and trusted colleague

*   *   *   *   *

'For the gifts and calling of God
are without repentance"
Romans 11:29

The Hope of Glory

An Exposition of The Eighth Chapter in
The Epistle to The Romans

by

MARCUS L. LOANE

WORD BOOKS, Publishers
Waco, Texas

Acknowledgment

The author wishes to thank Thomas Nelson and Sons Ltd. for permission to use quotations from the *Revised Standard Version of the Bible,* copyrighted 1946 and 1952.

Contents

INTRODUCTION

This great chapter is the crowning passage in the Pauline thesis on the guilt of man and the grace of God. It is imperative, for this reason alone, to understand its connection with the earlier discussion, and there are two main schools of thought on this question. One school believes that the first verse marks a fresh start and that it is meant to restate the doctrine of justification; and the other school holds that the first verse follows straight on from the seventh chapter and that it is meant to pursue the doctrine of sanctification.

It is argued by the first school of thought that a proper exegesis of the text proves that this chapter begins afresh with a ringing declaration of the results of man's personal acceptance with God: "There is therefore now no condemnation to them which are in Christ Jesus: for in Christ Jesus the law of the Spirit of life made me free from the law of sin and death" (8:1-2).[1] These words are a fresh and independent affirmation of the basic doctrine which this letter expounds. They do not look back to any single passage as their immediate antecedent. They are meant to sum up the whole of the previous discussion so as to pave the way for a magnificent review of the security of all who are "called to be saints" (1:7).

It is argued by the other school of thought that the whole literary structure of the text is interrupted by its artificial separation into chapters. This is thought to obscure the fact that the long self-analysis in the seventh chapter has its immediate sequel in the exultation which fills the eighth chapter. The former is only relieved by a single fragment of hope towards its close: "O wretched man that I am! who shall deliver me from the body of this death? I thank God through Jesus Christ our Lord" (7:24-5). The latter is buoyant with praise from the

---

[1] R.V. The word order is slightly rearranged.

moment when it begins with its mighty saying: "There is therefore now no condemnation to them which are in Christ Jesus" (8:1). It is easy to think that the problems in the seventh chapter were caught up and answered in the glorious certainty which shines throughout the next chapter, and then it is as though a long starless night were followed by a golden summer morning.

And yet, however attractive this last view may for the moment appear, it is based on very superficial exegesis and cannot stand rigorous scrutiny. There are solid reasons, rooted in the grammar and the context of the initial paragraph in this chapter, which prove that the first school of thought is right. St. Paul paused in his stride and stood back to survey the whole landscape which had now been traversed. This was enough to evoke his verdict that there is no condemnation to them which are in Christ Jesus, because in Christ Jesus they were set free from sin and death. Then he resumed the march of thought and pressed forward to new summits of understanding and experience: for those "whom he justified, them he also glorified" (8:30).

The first reason for this verdict is based on the character of the particle *therefore* (8:1). This word in the English version is used for two different particles in the Greek text,[1] and the subtle shades of meaning which were clear in the manuscript are lost in the translation. One word is less positive, while the other is quite dogmatic. The former is inferential; the latter is syllogistic. In the first case, the force of the logic is tacit; in the next case, the strength of the saying is causal. The one indicates no more than a general inference from facts already established; and the other indicates what is now the obvious conclusion based on definite premises. It is the first and less emphatic particle which St. Paul used in this passage, and it is not meant to refer to one particular antecedent in the previous discussion. It sums up the whole trend of the earlier argument as

[1] ἄρα, οὖν.

the New English Bible so clearly suggests: "The conclusion of the matter is this."

The next reason for this verdict is based on the character of the substantive *condemnation* (8:1).[1] It is a term derived from the law-courts and it forms a judicial metaphor in the Pauline treatment of sin and grace. This means that the first verse refers to the judicial acceptance with God of all who are in Christ Jesus. This is totally different from the spirit of self-condemnation which pervades the seventh chapter, nor can it be treated as in direct continuance from that chapter at all. It is meant to reiterate the great foundational doctrine of man's judicial acceptance with God through faith in Christ as the only basis for man's growth in personal sanctity. This is strengthened by the evidence of the manuscripts as to the phrase "who walk not after the flesh, but after the Spirit": these words do not belong to the first verse at all, but were wrongly borrowed, out of context, from their rightful place in the fourth verse. The strict reading of the first verse shows that it deals with one subject alone: that is, how men can stand before the bar of God, not how they are to walk in His presence.

The third reason for this verdict is based on the character of the expression *hath made free* (8:2). This verb is used in the aorist tense[2] and should be rendered strictly as the Revised Version translates, *made free*. It states a fact, something that took place or was done at a given moment, a definite *fait accompli*. It is part of St. Paul's explanation as to why there is "no condemnation to them which are in Christ Jesus": this is because in Christ Jesus they are set free from all the claims of sin and death. That great work of deliverance was a distinct event, something complete, an act which now lay in the past. It is therefore quite wrong to isolate verse two from its context and to quote it as though it were in direct sequence from the brief thanksgiving towards the close of the seventh chapter (7:25). That brief fragment had been followed by a further statement which had summed up the whole review of man's

[1] κατάκριμα. [2] ἠλευθέρωσέν.

inner conflict in that chapter, and there is a complete break in the line of thought before the new chapter begins. And the aorist tense of this verb confirms the fact that this chapter begins with a fresh and conclusive assertion of the results of man's judicial acceptance with God: there is now *no condemnation* because he had been *made free* by an act of grace.

We may therefore conclude that this chapter forms a distinctive entity in the construction of the epistle: it fits into the thought structure and the literary framework as in itself a whole. All the early chapters are part of the background, and the seventh chapter supplies its own special motive. The whole line of thought from the first affirmation of the Gospel as the power of God to save (1:16) down to the final recognition of man's own inability (7:25) must have been in the mind of St. Paul as he voiced his thoughts aloud while his scribe wrote them down. But he made a fresh start in this chapter; he began *de novo* with a verse that summed up all his basic theology of grace. This new start marks the place where the various rivulets of the previous discussion all meet and merge in the mighty river of truth, and he proceeds to show how that river flows on towards the ocean of glory. The eighth chapter is the apex in the structure of the previous argument, yet it has an intrinsic unity which is of great value. It is the crown of that Pauline theology which has stamped its mark on the Church down the ages, and it invites quiet and independent study. It follows the Pilgrim from the moment when his burden is rolled off at the Cross to the moment when he is called to go in through the gates of the City where he will see the King: it shows that the man for whom there is no condemnation because he is in Christ Jesus (8:1) is that man whom neither life nor death can sever from the love that has no equal in Christ Jesus our Lord (8:39).

CHAPTER ONE

No Condemnation

"There is therefore now no condemnation to them which are in Christ Jesus." (A.V.)

"There is therefore now no condemnation to them that are in Christ Jesus." (R.V.)

"There is therefore now no condemnation for those who are in Christ Jesus." (R.S.V.).

—Romans 8:1

St. Paul might well have felt the need to pause after the penetrating self-analysis of the seventh chapter, and the scribe would wait in silence until he was ready to start again; but then his words were to scale the heights of glorious certainty and he was to survey the length and breadth of the land of divine promise. The long previous argument was the necessary preparation for this climax whose advent is announced with a ringing declaration of the fundamental doctrine in the theology of grace. It was brief but comprehensive and it would plant both feet on the rock of impregnable security: "There is therefore now no condemnation to them which are in Christ Jesus." The Authorised Version adds a phrase by way of definition: "who walk not after the flesh, but after the Spirit". These words are not found at the end of this verse in later versions, and the manuscript evidence shows that they were not part of the original Greek text. They are a gloss, borrowed from the fourth verse by a scribe who failed to appreciate St. Paul's mighty dictum. The first sentence in this chapter is a manifesto so plain and so forceful that it does not even allow for a verb in the Greek, and the word *is* appears in the English versions only for the sake of literary smoothness. The strength of this manifesto may be better conveyed by means of a suitable paraphrase: "So then, in full view of God's grace, there is now no adverse sentence for those who are by faith in Christ Jesus."

Pauline logic makes it essential for his readers to grasp the real sense of the word *therefore*.[1] This word means that, in view of the facts which have been argued out in detail, one may safely come to a conclusion; logic makes the final verdict self-evident. This argument from inference derives further strength from the fact that the definite particle is linked with a second word, *now*.[2] This word is not a note of time; it is a means of stress in a closely argued thesis. The force of the united expression is made clearer in an amplified paraphrase: so then; as things now are; in these circumstances. It shows how this verse fits into the whole structure of thought in the early chapters. It sums up what has gone before with the boldness of a recognised axiom and serves as a preface to the ultimate conclusion. It was in view of all the facts which had emerged from the previous argument that St. Paul could go on to state his case; and his case was that no condemnation is now in force for those who are in Christ Jesus.

The word *condemnation*[3] means that judicial overtones are heard once more; the metaphor is forensic. The word itself occurs only twice in the New Testament apart from this verse, and each occurrence is found in this epistle (5:16, 18). But the cognate verb is frequent;[4] it means "to pass sentence of death" (cf. Mark 16:16; 1 Cor. 11:32). This is the sense in which the noun is used in the contrast between "condemnation" as a result of one man's fall and "justification" as a result of another man's righteousness: "Therefore, as by the offence of one, judgment came upon all men to condemnation, even so, by

[1] ἄρα. [2] νῦν. [3] κατάκριμα. [4] κατακρίνω.

the righteousness of one, the free gift came upon all men for justification" (5:18). A man may be accused of an offence, arraigned before a judge and found guilty; then the sentence will be pronounced and his doom will follow. *Condemnation* does not refer to the verdict that declares him guilty; it points to the sentence of death. It is only when the accusation is proved that a verdict of guilt can be pronounced: but that verdict must result in condemnation. The moment of condemnation is when sentence of death is passed, and that sentence has its sequel in the act of execution.

This clears the way for the mighty declaration: "There is therefore now *no condemnation* to them which are in Christ Jesus." Condemnation is what all men deserve: they have all sinned (3:23) and the wages of sin is death (6:23). But St. Paul took his stand on the *terra firma* of all that God in Christ has wrought, and this taught him to shout the great good news that there is *no condemnation* for those who are in Christ Jesus. That word *no* is as great as it is brief;[1] it stands first with emphatic prominence in the Greek text, and it declares that God has placed those who are in union with Christ on ground where they will never be condemned. It does not mean that they have done nothing worthy of condemnation, but that in Him they will not be exposed to condemnation. This speaks of their legal standing in the sight and judgment of God, and it looks far beyond any given moment of time to their ultimate destiny. What though sin should demand condemnation? In Him they have been placed beyond its reach. They "shall not come into condemnation,[2] but (have) passed from death unto life" (John 5:24).

Paul's usage also makes it essential for his readers to grasp the real sense of the words *in Christ Jesus*. This phrase unlocks a vast realm of spiritual thought and experience; in the context of this letter, it represents a transition from the legal concept of a guilty

---

[1] Briefer in English than in Greek: οὐδὲν: [2] κρίσις.

sinner before his judge to the mystic ideal of a vital union with Christ. The whole previous argument makes it clear that those who have been "justified by faith" (5:1) are those who are described in this verse as *in Christ Jesus*. The phrase itself had twice been used in a doctrinal connection, and each case bears on the same point: "Being justified freely by his grace through the redemption that is *in Christ Jesus*" (3:24); "The free gift of God is eternal life *in Christ Jesus* our Lord" (6:23 R.V.). But the early chapters contain only one verse in which it is used with a strong personal reference: "Even so, reckon ye also yourselves to be dead unto sin, but alive unto God *in Christ Jesus*" (6:11 R.V.). This phrase only begins to stand out with luminous interest in the course of this new chapter when St. Paul took up the thought of union with Him. The phrase itself is used three times in this chapter and twice in the later chapters (8:1, 2, 39; 15:17; 16:3), while the shorter form, *in Christ,* is found no less than five times (9:1; 12:5; 16:7, 9, 10).

Those who have been reckoned righteous at the bar of divine judgment are now identified as those who are *in Christ Jesus*; they are incorporate in Him. This concept of union with Him has two distinct aspects: it is federal in the sense that they are in Him as all men were in Adam; it is organic in the sense that they are in Him as the branch is in the vine. Evan Hopkins found an illustration of what this means in an analogy from the laws of nature.[1] A bar of iron in its primitive condition is cold and dull and hard; but let it be placed in the fire and it will soon become a glowing and pliant piece of metal. The iron does not cease to be iron, and the fire does not cease to be fire; but the iron is suffused with the fire so that one cannot be separated from the other. So too man's soul in its natural

[1] Evan H. Hopkins: *The Law of Liberty in The Spiritual Life*, p. 38. It is interesting to note that the analogy of the fire and the iron was used by Martin Luther in 1520 to illustrate his concept of the real presence in the bread and the wine after consecration. See A. G. Dickens: *The English Reformation*, p. 62.

condition is cold and hard and dead; but let it be joined with Christ and it will soon vibrate with a new and glowing vitality. The man does not cease to be man and Christ does not cease to be Christ; but the life of God in the soul of man is such that the one cannot be separated from the other. True identity is retained, while union is complete: their properties are interchanged; their interests are interlocked. The man who is *in Christ Jesus* is united and solidary with Him, incorporate in Him, and in virtue of this union, he shares all the benefits of His "so great salvation" (Heb. 2:3).

Thus the logic in St. Paul's mind was this: there is now no prospect of that fatal condemnation in the case of those who have come into such a union with Him; God cannot pass sentence of death on those who are *in Christ Jesus* because all that is His has been reckoned as theirs. It is this fact that lies at the heart of the most astonishing declaration which he ever made with regard to Christ and the sinner: "He hath made him to be sin for us, who knew no sin; that we (who have no righteousness) might be made the righteousness of God in him" (2 Cor. 5:21). He was *for us* in the place of condemnation; we are *in him* where all condemnation has spent its force. He took what was ours as though it were His, and gave what was His as though it were ours. What He was not, that He became, so that we might become what we were not. It was in fact because He knew no sin that He could be made sin *for us*; and now it is because we are *in him* that we have no condemnation to fear. It is as a result of this reciprocal exchange that God clears the guilty, and this is what He does for all who are *in Christ Jesus*.

Perhaps the most versatile of all the great Elizabethans was Sir Walter Raleigh: courtier, soldier, sailor, explorer, scientist, poet, author, historian. It was his misfortune that he outlived the great queen when she died in March 1603. Four months later, he was suddenly imprisoned on a very doubtful charge of treason. His trial took place in the following November: he was condemned to death, and the scaffold was set up in the grounds of the Tower of London. He wrote what he believed would be his last letter to his wife; a poem followed.[1] He had denied the charge of high treason, and he now stands acquitted at the bar of history. But in the Tower he could only look up to the "bribeless hall" of heaven where the King's attorney is none other than Christ Himself:

> "And when the grand twelve-million jury
>   Of our sins, with direful fury,
> Against our souls black verdicts give,
>   Christ pleads His death, and then we live."

Raleigh's fate was postponed, and his execution did not take place until 1616; but when at last he was required to die beneath the axe, he met that death with an unfaltering faith and courage. He had grasped in essence the great fundamental meaning of the Pauline theology of grace: "There is therefore now *no condemnation* to them which are *in Christ Jesus.*"

[1] Cf. Norman Lloyd Williams: *Sir Walter Raleigh*, p. 209.

CHAPTER TWO

Made Free

"For the law of the Spirit of life in Christ Jesus hath made me free from the law of sin and death." (A.V.)

"For the law of the Spirit of life in Christ Jesus made me free from the law of sin and of death." (R.V.)

"For the law of the Spirit of life in Christ Jesus has set me free from the law of sin and death." (R.S.V.)

Romans 8:2

This text travels on from the first verse to explain the great secret of such freedom from all condemnation, and the well-known Pauline word *for* is the link in the chain of thought. The full meaning of this emphatic connection has been obscured to some extent because the main factor in the logic of this passage is the significant repetition of the key phrase *in Christ Jesus*. The word order seems to allow this phrase in the second verse to be linked either with the subject, "the law of the Spirit of life", or with the verb, "hath made me free". But the absence of a connecting particle[1] before the phrase *in Christ Jesus* makes it clear that these words ought to go with the verb rather than the subject. This means that they form a distinct unit in the literary structure of this passage: they were caught up from the first verse and used again in a way which governs the thought of

[1] τῆς.

17

the whole text. This can be seen at once in a simple rearrange-ment of word order: "There is therefore now no condemnation to them which are *in Christ Jesus:* for *in Christ Jesus* the law of the Spirit of life hath made me free from the law of sin and death." There is now no condemnation because we have been made free from the law of sin and death: and this freedom has been wrought by the law of the Spirit of life as a result of our union with Christ Jesus. The whole process is in Him "who of God is made unto us wisdom" both for righteousness and for redemption.

What is *the law of sin,* and how does it fit into the general argument? It is a phrase which St. Paul had used to sum up one strange effect of the mysterious dualism which he perceived in his nature: "So then with the mind I myself serve the law of God; but with the flesh *the law of sin*" (7:25). There were two laws at work in his inmost being, and they were in violent collision. The law of God required him to do what was right; the law of sin compelled him to do what was wrong. St. Paul found that he was crippled by a double lack of ability: he could neither fulfil the law of God, nor yet escape the law of sin. The fact that he perceived the law of God only served to provoke the law of sin; he could not do what God required, and this meant that sin took on a yet more definite character. Thus there is a subtle sequence of thought in the choice of this phrase. It is the law of God, just and holy and good, which stands in the background; and that law now provokes the law of sin by "the unrelieved collision" of its absolute holiness with man's self-will.[1] *The law of sin* is a phrase that denotes the fixed process of man's revolt against the law of God as a result of his fallen self-will.

But why is this law also aligned with the law of *death*? This is because death is the wage of sin, and they are both equally con-nected with the work of the law of God. This is clearly ex-

[1] H. C. G. Moule: *The Epistle to the Romans* (The Expositors' Bible), p. 211.

pressed in St. Paul's words elsewhere: "For the letter killeth" (2 Cor. 3:6). St. Paul conceived of the letter of the law as something which by its own nature must lie outside man's heart, and its primary reference was to the law which God had set before Israel on Mount Sinai. That law had been engraved on two tables of stone; it was never engraved on the heart of Israel. It was always like a written letter which the ancient Hebrew could read, and it always remained outside his own inmost spirit. Israel knew the law of God as it was engraved on the tables of stone; there are others who may know it only as it has been written on their conscience. But it does not matter in what degree or what manner that law is known; it is under that law that all men stand. The law of God speaks with one voice: "This do, and thou shalt live" (Luke 10:28). It is not the hearer, but the doer of the law who shall live, and he who is guilty in one point is guilty in all. Alas! "There is none righteous, no, not one . . . There is none that doeth good, no, not one" (3:10, 12). Thus the letter killeth, for a broken law can only cry out for the sentence of death.

The law of sin and death casts a sombre shadow on theology and experience alike. Sin is always lethal; it was as a result of sin that death first came into the world (5:12). "I was alive apart from the law once," St. Paul declared, "but when the commandment came, sin revived, and I died" (7:9 R.V.). The law had been ordained with a view to life as its prize, but he found that it had become the cause of death. And the logic in his thinking is clear: the law by its very nature provokes the sharp revolt of sin; then it provides the stern warrant of death. "Did then that which is good become death unto me? God forbid. But sin, that it might be shewn to be sin, by working death to me through that which is good" (7:13 R.V.). God is holy, and must command; man is fallen, and must rebel. God is righteous, and must condemn; man is guilty, and must submit. Thus sin is man's revolt against the law of God, and death stalks the footsteps of sin like a hunter who must slay the outlaw. *The law of sin and death* is not a mere figure of speech: it is frightening; it is threatening; it is the stark reality which stares man in the face unless he is *in Christ Jesus.*

What is *the law of the Spirit,* and how does it fit into the general argument? The long analysis in the seventh chapter of man's struggle with sin had been steeped in his own selfish ego. St. Paul had written in the first person throughout, and the pronoun occurs eight times in the Greek text with all the weight of an emphatic utterance.[1] The name of God's Holy Spirit was not once heard in that context; his eyes were turned inward and there was no vision of the divine agent of grace. But there is a vast change in this chapter, for the Holy Spirit is named in no less than thirteen verses while His presence and power are felt from first to last.[2] It is true that *the law of the Spirit* did not emerge without some slight prior notice; His name and work had been briefly mentioned in the early chapters (1:4; 5:5; see also 2:29; 7:6). Such a notice was slender indeed, but it served its purpose. A man may put his ear to the ground in limestone country and catch the sound of the buried waters before they burst into the light of day: so too may we in these verses catch the first hint of that unseen presence before *the law of the Spirit* at last breaks out into full view in this chapter.[3]

But why is this law also aligned with the law of *life?* This is because life is the gift of the Spirit, and they are both equally related to the work of the grace of God. This is clearly expressed in St. Paul's words elsewhere: "The Spirit giveth life" (2 Cor. 3:6). It has sometimes been thought that *the Spirit* in this context only refers to the spirit of the law as opposed to its letter; but a careful study of the terms of Pauline theology

[1] ἐγώ 7:9 (twice), 14, 17, 20 (twice), 24, 25.

[2] πνεῦμα 8:2, 4, 5 (twice), 6, 9 (three times), 11 (twice), 13, 14, 15 (twice), 16, 23, 26 (twice), 27.

[3] H. C. G. Moule: op. cit., p. 204.

leaves no room for doubt that St. Paul meant the Spirit of God.[1] Fallen sinful man bears in his nature the marks of death: he is dead in sin; he is dead to God. His most urgent need is for the experience of a new birth and the gift of new life. This is the work of God's Holy Spirit in the inmost region of man's being, for He alone is the author of that newness of life which makes men new creatures in Christ Jesus. The new birth means life that is "born of the Spirit" (John 3:6); that life is His gift "from above" (John 3:3 R.V.M.). Therefore St. Paul could speak of *the Spirit of life* just as he had spoken of "the Spirit of holiness" (1:4) There is one small point of grammar in his saying about "the law of the Spirit *of* life" in mild contrast with that of his saying about "the law of sin *and* death"; but this genitive expression rather than the regular conjunction adds strength to the idea that the Holy Spirit is the unique author of all such life.

The law of the Spirit of life is a phrase of tremendous paradox coined by St. Paul to clinch his point. The law and the Spirit at first sight seem to be rivals; yet in this verse St. Paul boldly applied the word *law* to the work of grace. This is comparable with a similar paradox in an earlier expression: "The law of faith" (3:27). The act of grace by which a man is freed from all condemnation is in God's sight "a law in the sense of a fixed process".[2] The law of grace is seen at work when God bestows the gift of life on the man who is born of the Spirit: this is the rule by which God is pleased to carry out His work in the soul of man. It was not as though St. Paul meant to point to some new and better Gospel of the Spirit; his thought did not for one moment advance from the dispensation of the Lord Christ to some higher region controlled by

[1] H. C. G. Moule treats the word throughout Romans chapter eight as a reference to the Holy Spirit except in verse 10 and once in verse 16 when it refers to the human spirit. See *The Epistle to the Romans* (The Cambridge Bible), p. 140.   [2] H. C. G. Moule: ibid., p. 137.

the Holy Spirit.[1] *The law of the Spirit of life* is no independent separable blessing: it is basic to the Gospel; it spells freedom for those who are *in Christ Jesus*.

"The word *law* is . . . (thus) used in the sense of a fixed process in both parts of the verse"[2] and the contrast is like that between "the ministration of death" and "the ministration of the Spirit" elsewhere (2 Cor. 3:7,8). The New Covenant is linked by the chain of cause and effect with *the Spirit of life* just as the Old Covenant was linked with *sin and death*. It was with all this in full view that St. Paul made his great declaration: "There is therefore now no condemnation to them that are in Christ Jesus: for in Christ Jesus the law of the Spirit of life *made me free* (R.V.) from the law of sin and death." The verb in the aorist tense shows that this deliverance was a past act, a definite and accomplished reality, the great basic experience of those who are reckoned righteous by faith (5:1). St. Paul turned from the vague plural pronoun *them* to a strong personal reference in the word *me* (cf. Gal. 2:17–21). It is true that certain ancient authorities read *thee* rather than *me* (cf. N.E.B.); but Sanday and Headlam point out that the pronoun in the second person does not belong to the context at all and the reading *thee* is just "a mechanical repetition of the last syllable" in the Greek verb.[3] Who is this *me* but the man who had cried out in anguish "O wretched man that I am: who shall deliver me?" (7:24). The word in this new verse is an echo from that lament; the man of that conflict had been driven back to the great fundamental crisis of grace. The secret of freedom belongs to them that are in Christ Jesus; it is the law of the Spirit which makes them free.

[1] H. C. G. Moule: *Romans* (The Expositors' Bible), p. 206.
[2] H. C. G. Moule: *Romans* (The Cambridge Bible), p. 138.
[3] ἠλευθέρωσέν, cf. W. Sanday and A. C. Headlam: *The Epistle to the Romans*, p. 191.

CHAPTER THREE

An Offering for Sin

"For what the law could not do, in that it was weak
through the flesh, God sending his own Son in the
likeness of sinful flesh, and for sin, condemned sin
in the flesh: that the righteousness of the law might be
fulfilled in us, who walk not after the flesh, but after
the Spirit." (A.V.)

"For what the law could not do, in that it was weak
through the flesh, God, sending his own Son in the
likeness of sinful flesh and as an offering for sin,
condemned sin in the flesh: that the ordinance of the
law might be fulfilled in us, who walk not after the
flesh, but after the spirit." (R.V.)

"For God has done what the law, weakened by the
flesh, could not do: sending his own Son in the likeness of sinful flesh and for sin, he condemned sin in
the flesh, in order that the just requirement of the law
might be fulfilled in us, who walk not according to
the flesh but according to the Spirit." (R.S.V.)

—Romans 8:3–4

These words forge a new link in the chain of thought and
logic with which this great chapter begins, and they start with
a word which shows that their function was to expand the
meaning and to explain the process hinted at in the words
that go before. It is *in Christ Jesus* that we were set free from the

law of sin and death, *for* God has done on our behalf what the law could not do. The text is marked by a certain disjointed construction known to grammarians as anacoluthon: the sentence which begins in one way ends in another.[1] This means that it is best to treat the first phrase as an accusative absolute: "As to, or in view of, the inability of the law." What the law could not do was to set men free from the guilt and power of sin and help them to live by the rule of the Spirit. It could speak of duty, but it could not make men obey; it could condemn failure, but it could not secure freedom from the judgment which such failure deserved. It could not justify, it could not sanctify: that was not its function; it lay beyond its scope. It had no power to help men once they had become subject to sin and death. If men could but comply with its demands, it would count them righteous; but that is the very point in which the inability of the law consists. It is *weak through the flesh* and it can do nothing as a result of our fallen nature. "St. Paul guards the honour of the law" (cf. 7:7),[2] and lays on man the blame for failure. He makes it clear that the source of failure does not lie in the law as such, but in man as sinful. Therefore since the law can secure neither the spirit of obedience nor release from condemnation, God sent forth His own Son to set men free from the sentence of death and to give them power to live by the Spirit.

The great doctrinal emphasis at the heart of this text is based on the reality of the Incarnation; *God sending forth his own Son in the likeness of sinful flesh and for sin.* The name of God is brought into the text with an impressive awareness of its value as a factor in the unfolding argument; but it is not to be treated as if it were in some kind of opposition to the word *law.* God is the source of the law which came by Moses just as truly as

[1] A. M. Hunter: *The Epistle to The Romans* (The Torch Bible Commentaries), p. 79.
[2] H. C. G. Moule: *Romans* (The Cambridge Bible), p. 138.

He is the source of the grace which came by Christ. But the God who gave the law is under view in this text as the God of all grace, for grace did what law could not do when God sent forth His Son. He did not send a mere angel spirit or an ordinary person on this mission; He sent the one who was most near and dear as the Son of His love. The brief phrase *his own Son* may be compared with a subsequent reference in this chapter (8:32). The Greek is not identical;[1] the emphasis is similar. It points to the unique nature of the Father and the Son as members of the triune Godhead; it points just as clearly to the divine nearness between the one who gave and the one who was thus given. God's *own Son* had shared His love and glory before the worlds were made, but the time came when God sent Him in the fulness of grace to live as man with men. "God so loved the world that He gave" the best that He could give in the person of "His only begotten Son" (John 3:16).

St. Paul's words were chosen with no small care when he referred to the Incarnation: God sent His Son *in the likeness of sinful flesh*. He might have been content to say that He came "in the flesh", just as St. John declared that "the Word was made flesh" (John 1:14); but he wanted to stress the fact that He was clothed with our human nature without the taint of sin. Therefore his phrase elaborates and defines the form in which He came, and each word is significant. He did not say *in the likeness of flesh,* for that would have implied that His flesh was unreal; and it could not be said that He had come as a spirit or a phantom might come, with only the semblance of a body. Nor did he say *in sinful flesh,* for that would have implied that He was not immune from sin; and it could not be said that He had come with a nature that was defiled by the latent presence of sin. St. Paul's language is as exact as words can be; God sent His Son *in the likeness of sinful flesh:* His was, like ours, a true human body, yet in Him was no sin at all. He took

[1] τὸν ἑαυτοῦ Υἱὸν (8:3) τοῦ ἰδίου Υἱοῦ (8:32).

real flesh, the flesh which is for us hardly separable from sin. He was exposed to all the needs and trials and pains of our nature which sin brought in its train. He felt the strain of all that in our case often leads on to sin, yet sin found no foothold in Him at all. Therefore St. Paul declared that He came in a form which was *like* our sinful nature, and yet only *like* because not itself sinful.

St. Paul then summed up in two words the great object of this Divine mission: God sent His Son into the world *for sin.* The Greek preposition[1] could mean no more than that He was sent *on account of sin,* leaving a more precise definition undetermined; but it is used in the Septuagint with a special sacrificial significance. Thus Sanday and Headlam note that it is employed more than fifty times in Leviticus alone with reference to sacrifice.[2] This use is adopted in the New Testament when the discussion adverted to "sacrifice and offering *for sin*" (Heb. 10:6,8,18), and the context demands the same meaning for the word in this phrase (cf. Rom. 3:25). This can only mean that God sent Him as *a sin-offering* (Num. 8:8) or *a sacrifice for sin* (N.E.B.). The doom of *sin* must fall on *sinful flesh*; that doom is death: but God sent His Son *in the flesh* that He might bear that doom for us. No angel could suffer for man; no mere spirit could bleed and die: only one who shared our flesh and blood and yet who knew no sin could die as a sin-offering and a sacrifice for sin. Therefore the Son of God took man's very nature that He might bear the doom which that nature deserves because of sin.

The strong practical emphasis at the heart of this text is based on the reality of sin's condemnation: *God . . . condemned sin in the flesh that the righteousness of the law might be fulfilled in us.* There is now no condemnation for those who are in Him because in Him God has condemned their sin. Sin as such is

---

[1] περί.

[2] W. Sanday and A. C. Headlam: op. cit., p. 193.

never pardoned; it is condemned. The sentence of condemnation has been pronounced and the judgment which it entailed has been executed. Sin was worthy of death and was punished as it deserved. And this took place in the person of God's own Son; sin was judged *in the flesh*. It was not put away merely by a verbal fiat or an abstract satisfaction; it was nailed to the cross and done to death in Christ Himself on that hill of shame and disgrace. God could only provide pardon for the sinner as a result of the condemnation of sin in one who was called to bear the sin of the world. What man deserves in his sinful nature was borne for him in the sinless nature of the man, Christ Jesus. Fallen man's sin was both judged and punished in the perfect manhood of the Incarnate Redeemer. The main force of St. Paul's language is the idea of penalty and punishment which have been put into execution. God rose up in judgment to put an end to sin when He laid it all on His Son. He was made to be sin for us (2 Cor. 5:21); He had to bear the curse which sin deserves (Gal. 3:13). He was condemned that no condemnation should fall on those who are in Him; His death as the penal reward for sin was the necessary price of freedom for us.

St. Paul at once makes it clear that this was done in order that *the righteousness of the law might be fulfilled in us*. Sin was condemned and the penalty exacted in the person of Christ with a view to a new obedience on the part of those who are now in Him. The word *righteousness* is used in this context as the antithesis of the word *condemnation* (cf. 5:16,18).[1] It is not the ordinary word used in Greek,[2] and it reflects its own special shade of meaning. It points to that which is laid down as right, or has the force of right, and in this phrase, it can only refer to the statutes of law.[3] *The righteousness of the law* represents the requirements of the law; it stands for the claims of the law on

---

[1] δικαίωμα, κατάκριμα. [2] δικαιοσύνη.
[3] W. Sanday and A. C. Headlam: op. cit., p. 194.

all mankind. The law of God had to be satisfied if men were to be justified: this would have been impossible were it not for what God in Christ has done. Thus his tremendous argument is that God has condemned sin in the flesh so that all the righteous demands of the law may be met in the case of all who are in union with Him. The same astonishing doctrine shines through another tremendous Pauline statement which can never be too deeply pondered: "He hath made him to be sin for us, who knew no sin; that we might be made the righteousness of God in him" (2 Cor. 5:21).

St. Paul concludes with a phrase which shows what manner of life will mark the man who is in Christ Jesus: he will *walk not after the flesh, but after the Spirit*. These words look beyond the fact of righteousness and point to the need for holiness; they are firm proof that the doctrines of grace have no anti-nomian characteristics. "Those only are justified who are also sanctified";[1] God is only right with those who are right with Him. Therefore those who have been set free from the fear of condemnation will bend all their efforts towards true holiness and harmony with Him. They will *walk, not after the flesh, but after the Spirit*; words that find an echo in the exhortation that if we live by the Spirit, we ought also to walk by the Spirit (Gal. 5:25). St. Paul borrowed an Old Testament metaphor for his picture of the regulation of man's life as a walk and placed the flesh and the Spirit in strong contrast as the two great ruling factors. God has met all the claims of the law for our sake, so that we may disown the rule of the flesh and may learn to live in the spirit of Enoch and Noah who "walked with God" (Gen. 5:24; 6:9).

The great Latin Father, Jerome, has left a clear record of the way in which he tried to obey the law and to subdue the flesh in his own strength. He lived as a hermit alone in the desert and gave himself up to weeks of fasting; but he had to

[1] Charles Hodge: *Commentary on The Epistle to The Romans*, p. 253.

confess at last that he could not banish the dark passions which were always ready to haunt his mind. "How often," so he wrote to Eustochium, "when I was living in the desert, parched by a burning sun, did I fancy myself among the pleasures of Rome! Sackcloth disfigured my unshapely limbs, and my skin from long neglect had become as black as an Ethiopian's ... And although in my fear of hell I had consigned myself to this prison, where I had no companions but scorpions and wild beasts, I often thought myself amid bevies of girls. My face was pale, and my frame chilled with fasting; yet my mind was burning with desire, and the fires of lust kept bubbling up before me when my flesh was as good as dead. Helpless, I cast myself at the feet of Jesus."[1] Jerome found that only one thing could meet his need; nothing could take its place. God was willing to do for him what he could not do for himself: he had to cast himself, helpless, at the feet of Jesus.

[1] See T. W. Drury: "Jerome", chapter fourteen in *Church Leaders in Primitive Times,* edited by William Lefroy, 1896, p. 462.

CHAPTER FOUR

The Mind of the Flesh

"For they that are after the flesh do mind the things of the flesh; but they that are after the Spirit the things of the Spirit. For to be carnally minded is death; but to be spiritually minded is life and peace. Because the carnal mind is enmity against God: for it is not subject to the law of God, neither indeed can be. So then they that are in the flesh cannot please God." (A.V.)

"For they that are after the flesh do mind the things of the flesh; but they that are after the spirit the things of the spirit. For the mind of the flesh is death; but the mind of the spirit is life and peace: Because the mind of the flesh is enmity against God; for it is not subject to the law of God, neither indeed can it be: And they that are in the flesh cannot please God."   (R.V.)

"For those who live according to the flesh set their minds on the things of the flesh, but those who live according to the Spirit set their minds on the things of the Spirit. To set the mind on the flesh is death, but to set the mind on the Spirit is life and peace. For the mind that is set on the flesh is hostile to God; it does not submit to God's law, indeed it cannot; and those who are in the flesh cannot please God."   (R.S.V.)

Romans 8:5–8

The last phrase in verse four provides a new point of departure in the discussion, and St. Paul now enters upon a strong dissertation about the flesh and the Spirit. The word *flesh* may be used in a figurative sense with one or other of two meanings. It is neutral when it refers to man's human nature as conditioned by the body (cf. 9:3,5,8); it is evil when it refers to man's nature as conditioned by the Fall (cf. 7:5,18,25). The *flesh* in the latter sense is indicative of the power of sin which works so largely through the bodily conditions of life; it is that element which strives to resist the grace of God, whether before or after man becomes regenerate.[1] On the other hand, the *Spirit* in this chapter refers to God's Holy Spirit except in two verses where it refers to man's human spirit (cf. 8:10,16). It is not that man's own spirit is dislodged or displaced when he becomes regenerate; it is rather that God's Holy Spirit must indwell and control that now regenerate human spirit. This means that the controlling influence in such a man is the Spirit of God working in and through his regenerate spirit.[2] St. Paul therefore in this passage describes the *flesh* and the *Spirit* as two rival forces which both strive for control in man's inmost being. The *flesh* is the evil bias in a nature "vitiated by sin",[3] and the *Spirit* is the divine agent in a nature regenerate through grace. This is comparable with his statement in a companion epistle on the divine law of counter-action: "The flesh lusteth against the Spirit, and the Spirit against the flesh: and these are contrary the one to the other" (Gal. 5:17).

St. Paul begins with the antithesis between the flesh and the Spirit: *for they that are after the flesh do mind the things of the flesh.* The word *for* connects this verse with the last phrase and makes it clear that its purpose is to show why freedom from condemnation is confined to those who now "walk not after the flesh,

---

[1] H. C. G. Moule: op. cit., p. 140.
[2] Ibid. pp. 140-1.
[3] A. M. Hunter: op. cit., p. 79.

but after the Spirit" (8:4). To walk after the flesh is the outward sign and demonstration of those who *are* after the flesh;
walking "flesh-wise" has its root in being "unchanged children
of the self-life".[1] Such are they who obey the flesh, make it
their rule, and yield to it as the organ of sin in spite of all
knowledge of right and wrong. They are further defined as
those who *do mind* the things of the flesh. The wide meaning of
this verb is made clear by its derivation from a term which
denotes the seat of all our faculties and affections.[2] It is much
more than to like or care for something; it means the full
occupation of the mind and the will with some all-engrossing
subject. It is to have moral affinity with, to set one's innermost
affections on, this or that (cf. Col. 3:2), and here it is applied
to *the things of the flesh*. Such things are not confined to what
speaks of sensual interest; they are all those things which do not
belong to the category described as "things that be of God"
(Matt. 16:23). They are "earthly things" (Phil. 3:19), not the
"things (that are) above" (Col. 3:2). Those who cling to the
flesh cannot help but choose the things of the flesh.

But the contrast is immediate and imperative: *but they that are
after the Spirit the things of the Spirit.* To be *after the Spirit* here
denotes those who have been awakened, illumined, by the
Holy Spirit and whose lives are governed by the fact that He
dwells in them. They set their mind upon *the things of the
Spirit* and are absorbed by this heavenly interest. They are
moved to "look not at the things which are seen, but at the
things which are not seen: for the things which are seen are
temporal, but the things which are not seen are eternal" (2 Cor.
4:18). This is not a matter of elation or emotion; it does not
point to some non-natural state of exaltation. It does not hint
at some kind of freedom from all inner conflict with sin (cf.
8:13) or trial (cf. 8:17), and it does not mean that men can

[1] H. C. G. Moule: *Romans* (The Expositor's Bible), p. 213.
[2] φϱονέω, φϱήν.

lose sight of the sufferings of the universe (8:22). It is just "a question of . . . the ambitions which compel us and the interests which engross us";[1] it points to a state of mind which tries to focus all its powers on the things that are above, and so hold converse with God in the Spirit. It is indeed what men think in their heart that comes out in their life; things which occupy their mind determine the whole bent of their will. And they that are after the Spirit cannot help but prefer the things of the Spirit.

St. Paul makes it clear that these two groups are totally alien to each other: *for the mind of the flesh is death, but the mind of the Spirit is life and peace* (R.V.). The word *for* shows that the sequence of thought lays stress on the profound reality of the contrast between the flesh and the Spirit: they are so far opposed to each other that the one ends in death while the other brings life and peace. The same kind of antithesis is found in the contrast between the *works* of the flesh and the *fruit* of the Spirit (Gal. 5:19,22). The *mind* of the flesh and the *mind* of the Spirit carry on the idea of the last verse with a cognate form of the verb.[2] It means a state of mind which is revealed in desire and pursuit of a congenial object. To set one's mind on the things of the flesh spells *death:* this can only mean "the ruin of the soul in condemnation and in separation from God".[3] The whole context helps to define *death* as the doom which falls on those who are under sentence: they are condemned in a legal sense as those who are hostile to the law of God (cf. 8:7), and in a moral sense as those who cannot please God (cf. 8:8). This is the *death* of the soul in as much as it means the absence of life; therefore "there can be no such thing as salvation in sin".[4] But to set one's mind on the things of the Spirit spells *life and peace,* and by analogy, this points to the welfare of the soul in

---

[1] J. R. W. Stott: *Life in the Spirit* (The Keswick Convention, 1965), p. 119.
[2] φρόνημα.   [3] H. C. G. Moule: op. cit., p. 213.
[4] Charles Hodge: op. cit., p. 254.

c

acquittal from sin and in acceptance with God. It speaks of the special aspect of forgiveness and fellowship with Him: for there is life in His favour, and His presence means peace (cf. Malachi 2:5).

St. Paul proceeds with an analysis of the mind of the flesh: *because the mind of the flesh is enmity against God* (R.V.). This phrase throws light on the radical difference between the two minds as described in the last verse and points out the basic reason why the mind of the flesh is so fatal. It is death as opposed to life; it is also war as opposed to peace. St. Paul chose a word which was as forceful as language could provide; it makes the whole saying comparable with the declaration that "the friendship of the world is *enmity* with God" (James 4:4).[1] The mind of the flesh is in frank revolt against the law of God; it is by its very nature hostile to Him who should be the life of the soul. This is the more easily understood if the great words are kept in mind: "Thou shalt love the Lord thy God with all thy heart, and with all thy soul, and with all thy mind" (Matt. 22:37; cf. Deut. 6:5). God makes His claim for the love of the whole of man's being, and the mind of the flesh is in direct conflict with such a claim. Therefore St. Paul describes it as personal enmity against the Lord our God; those who have the mind of the flesh and who pursue the things of the flesh are at war with Him. They may not be starkly conscious of such hostility, but it is the ruling factor at the seat of their soul.

This is further explained in words that sum up the defiant attitude of the mind of the flesh: *for it is not subject to the law of God, neither indeed can it be* (R.V.). The strong character of this expression finds a parallel in the emphasis which St. Paul placed on the ignorance of the natural man for the things of the Spirit in his other saying: "The natural man receiveth not the things of the Spirit . . . neither can he know them" (1 Cor. 2:14). St. Paul states the case with dogmatic energy in this

[1] Compare ἔχθρα εἰς Θεόν (Rom. 8:7) and ἔχθρα τοῦ Θεοῦ (James 4:4).

verse so as to leave no room for hesitant compromise. The mind of the flesh not only does not submit to the claims of the law; it is incapable of all genuine submission to God. It is in its very essence estranged from Him, hostile to Him, at war with Him. It has in its rebel nature the seed which by ordinary germination must bring forth death "both of soul and body, both here and hereafter".[1] This is why its outlook is as hopeless as the idea of death itself implies.

St. Paul concludes with a verdict which is marked by crystalline clarity: *so then they that are in the flesh cannot please God.* The brief connecting particle which the Authorised Version translates by the phrase *so then* is better rendered as *but* or *and* (R.V.) or else left out altogether (R.S.V.).[2] It does not mark a fresh point of logic, but paves the way for the final application of the last strong dogmatic utterance. They that are *in the flesh* in the moral sense of that phrase are in effect all those who are *after the flesh* (cf. 8:5), and such cannot please God. Perhaps the true meaning of New Testament holiness is never more clearly expressed than in St. Paul's exhortation "to walk and to please God" (1 Thess. 4:1) and the ideas of walking and pleasing both run through this passage. They sum up the chief end for which man was first made (cf. Rev. 4:11), and they were both exemplified in the life of the Son of Man who did always those things that were pleasing to His Father (cf. John 8:29). But the man who has the mind of the flesh *cannot please God*; it is beyond his power. The name of God has an emphatic position in the Greek text, and this heightens the strong sense of finality. The same finality sounds through another utterance on this subject: "Without faith it is impossible to please Him" (Heb. 11:6). This is not a harsh or narrow-minded dogma; it is a calm, deliberate statement of truth. The mind of the flesh will never choose God and make Him its

---

[1] W. Sanday and A. C. Headlam: op. cit., p. 195.   [2] δὲ.

supreme delight, for it is in implacable hostility to all His claims.

The grave dogmatic overtones of this verdict call for a pause; perhaps St. Paul himself would fall silent for a moment or two. Men can never please God if they fail to love Him with all their heart and soul and mind; and yet not to please Him is to forfeit His love and His favour. Thus man's enmity and God's displeasure are the concomitants whose end is death; the prospect is hopeless. Yet it is not unlike the old story of Faust who had gambled for his soul with Satan. Dr. James Stewart refers to the picture which shows a game of chess with Faust at one side and Satan at the other.[1] The game was as good as over: Faust had only a few pieces left, a king, a knight, one or two pawns. He had a look of blank despair while the devil had the leer of coming triumph. Many a chess player had looked at this picture and had agreed that the game was finished; it was checkmate. At length a great master of the game found himself absorbed in the drama, fascinated by Faust's look of haunting despair. His eyes went to the board and he stared at the few pieces which still remained. Other people came and went while he was immersed in thought. And suddenly the gallery rang with his shout: "It is a lie! The king and the knight have another move!" And this is true of the human struggle. It is hopeless where the mind of the flesh is concerned; but our God and His Son have another move.

[1] James S. Stewart: *A Faith to Proclaim*, p. 66.

CHAPTER FIVE

The Mind of the Spirit

"But ye are not in the flesh, but in the Spirit, if so be that the Spirit of God dwell in you. Now if any man have not the Spirit of Christ, he is none of his. And if Christ be in you, the body is dead because of sin; but the Spirit is life because of righteousness. But if the Spirit of him that raised up Jesus from the dead dwell in you, he that raised up Christ from the dead shall also quicken your mortal bodies by his Spirit that dwelleth in you." (A.V.)

"But ye are not in the flesh, but in the spirit, if so be that the Spirit of God dwelleth in you. But if any man hath not the Spirit of Christ, he is none of his. And if Christ is in you, the body is dead because of sin; but the spirit is life because of righteousness. But if the Spirit of him that raised up Jesus from the dead dwelleth in you, he that raised up Christ Jesus from the dead shall quicken also your mortal bodies through his Spirit that dwelleth in you." (R.V.)

"But you are not in the flesh, you are in the Spirit, if the Spirit of God really dwells in you. Any one who does not have the Spirit of Christ does not belong to him. But if Christ is in you, although your bodies are dead because of sin, your spirits are alive because of righteousness. If the Spirit of him who raised Jesus from the dead dwells in you, he who raised

Christ Jesus from the dead will give life to your
mortal bodies also through his Spirit which dwells
in you." (R.S.V.).

—Romans 8:9–11

St. Paul turns from the mind of the flesh to the mind of the
Spirit, and the exposition of the issues of death gives way to an
exposition of the issues of life. There are certain features in the
language of this passage which impinge on theology in a way
that calls for special comment at the outset. The first feature
has to do with the mind of the Spirit and shows itself in a
succession of synonyms. Thus *the Spirit of God* and *the Spirit
of Christ* follow each other as equivalent terms for the same
person (8:9). To be *in the Spirit* is the same thing as to have
the Spirit of God in you (8:9). And to have *the Spirit of God in
you* is to have *Christ in you* (8:10). This interchange of expressions is a remarkable testimony to St. Paul's strong Trinitarian
faith: there may be no formal treatment of this doctrine, but it
pervades all his thinking. The next feature has a bearing on the
issues of life and shows itself in a rising spiral of thought. Just
as death meant the death of the whole man, both in body and
in spirit, so life is meant for the whole man, both in spirit and
in body. St. Paul's thought climbs upward in a deliberate
ascent from the regenerate human spirit to the living Spirit of
God (8:10,11), and from the death of the mortal body to the
resurrection of that body by the power of the same Spirit (8:11).
The mind of the flesh is thus no more than a "dark foil" for
the mind of the Spirit,[1] and the life which the same Spirit
bestows will at length bring about the complete and final
conquest of death.

St. Paul turns from the third person (8:8) to the forms of
direct address as he takes up the mind of the Spirit, and this
change is marked by the warm personal emphasis on the

[1] H. C. G. Moule: *Romans* (The Cambridge Bible), p. 143.

word *you* in the Greek text: *but ye are not in the flesh, but in the Spirit, if so be that the Spirit of God dwell in you.* He had described them as *in Christ Jesus* (8:1); now he describes them as *in the Spirit.* So too St. John on the Isle of Patmos spoke of himself as one who was *in the Spirit* when he heard the voice from heaven (Rev. 1:10). This phrase cannot mean less than that they were enveloped in an atmosphere in which the one controlling influence was the Holy Spirit; the whole bent and bias of their life was governed by the realities of His presence and power. This would assume that the Spirit of God did in fact dwell in them, and the connecting particle, *if so be,*[1] makes this plain. It was not a mere *if;* it was meant to suggest only that element of misgiving which would result in true self-examination (cf. 2 Cor. 13:5). Elsewhere he had described sin as that which "dwelleth in me" (7:17,20); here he used the same word to speak of the Spirit of God who dwelt in them. Jesus Himself had said of the Spirit: "He dwelleth with you and shall be in you" (John 14:17). That He should *dwell* within points to something as intimate and permanent as language can convey. It speaks of a settled, enduring, "penetrative influence"[2] which cannot be separated from life on the level of the Spirit of God.

The next words are by way of parenthesis in order to prevent the false application of this profound teaching: *now if any man have not the Spirit of Christ, he is none of his.* This cool dogmatic utterance may be compared with its positive counterpart: "If any man be in Christ, he is a new creature" (2 Cor. 5:17). It is just as final as the words of the Son of Man (cf. John 3:3; Matt. 18:3); nothing at all is of any avail if this one great thing be lacking. But St. Paul puts this test forward with a delicacy which makes it both strong and gentle. He had assumed that the Spirit of God was now dwelling *in you,* that is, in each of them as individuals, and such language was personal and definite. But when he wished to state something in the form of

[1] *εἴπερ.* [2] W. Sanday and A. C. Headlam: op. cit., p. 196.

dogma, he cast his words, *if any man,* into a more general formula. And the point was whether or not a man has *the Spirit of Christ,* a phrase which has various parallels elsewhere (Gal. 4:6; Phil. 1:19; 1 Pet. 1:11). This makes it clear that the Holy Spirit is rightly represented as in intimate connection with Christ. Men need to be strengthened in their inmost being by means of the Spirit so that Christ may dwell in their hearts (Ephes. 3:16,17). But the phrase in this verse is all the more remarkable because of its proximity to the previous reference to *the Spirit of God.* This shows that He is *the Spirit of Christ* in the same sense that He is *the Spirit of God*; He holds the same personal relation to each. If then any man have not the Spirit of Christ, he is *none of His*; he does not *belong to Him* (R.S.V.). "Know ye not your own selves how that Jesus Christ is in you, except ye be reprobates?" (2 Cor. 13:5).

This brief warning is then followed by a return to the main theme: *and if Christ be in you, the body is dead because of sin.* This verse is in contrast with the dogma expressed in the last clause, and the connecting particle should be rendered by the word *but* (R.S.V.) rather than *and* (A.V., R.V.). The sense of the passage would then be that if a man have not the Spirit of Christ, he has no part in Him; *but* if Christ be in him, although his body is mortal, he shares with Him the true secret of life. The verse begins with the momentous transition from *the Spirit of Christ* to *Christ* Himself, and this is the fundamental prerequisite for the ensuing argument. The first step in the march of thought is in the phrase *the body is dead because of sin.* This offers no translation of a particle in the Greek text,[1] and a paraphrase helps to clarify the full meaning: "Your body, *it is true,* is doomed to death because it is tainted with sin."[2] St. Paul refers to man's mortal body, not to his flesh: the one shall yet be made alive (8:11), while the other must be nailed to the cross (Gal. 5:24). This meaning is required by the antithesis

---

[1] μὲν.   [2] W. Sanday and A. C. Headlam: op. cit., p. 195.

of body and spirit; it points to the body as that which is mortal, subject to death, "as good as dead" (4:19 R.V.). The word *dead*[1] is chosen rather than the word *mortal*[2] in order to provide an even more vivid contrast with the word *life*; it is *a dead thing* (N.E.B.). Such death is the penal result of sin (5:12; 6:23); it is *because of sin* that death first came into the world and that our now mortal bodies must die.

But this is in pointed contrast with God's purpose for those in whom Christ dwells: *but the Spirit is life because of righteousness*. Perhaps the force of this contrast can be better gauged through another translation: "Though the body is a dead thing, yet the spirit is life itself" (see N.E.B.). Older commentaries refer the word *Spirit* in this sentence to the human spirit on the ground that it is clearly opposed to the human body. This view was held by H. C. G. Moule in his first commentary,[3] but he changed his mind and argued later that the word must refer to the Holy Spirit on the ground that nothing less will suit the context and its grandeur of thought.[4] There can be no absolute conclusion, and the wise course may be to walk in the old paths.[5] St. Paul argues that the body has been consigned to the infection of death, while the spirit has been renewed by the infusion of life. The man in whom Christ dwells has been rescued from the spiritual death to which his spirit was prone; his now regenerate spirit has been quickened with that life which is from above. St. Paul's language means more than that it is alive; it means that its very essence is life. This strong contrast of the body as *a dead thing* and the spirit as *life itself* (N.E.B.) is a striking concept; it is carried even further in the final antithesis between death as the doom of sin, and life as the result of grace (cf. 8:6). The phrase *because of righteousness* must be interpreted

---

[1] νεκρόν. [2] θνητόν. [3] H. C. G. Moule: op. cit., p. 144.
[4] H. C. G. Moule: *Romans* (The Expositor's Bible), p. 214 fn.
[5] spirit (R.V.; R.S.V.; N.E.B.; Hodge; Sanday and Headlam; Moule [The Cambridge Bible]); Spirit (A.V.; Moule [The Expositor's Bible]; Bruce).

as the counterpart of the phrase *because of sin,* and it is "a practical synonym" for the work of justification.[1] This is made clear in the paraphrastic reading: "because you have been justified" (N.E.B.).

St. Paul's next words define his own concept of the Holy Spirit as one who is distinct from and yet in intimate connection with the other persons in the Godhead: *but if the Spirit of him that raised up Jesus from the dead dwell in you.* This clause starts with the same connecting particle with which the last verse had begun,[2] and then makes an almost surprising reference to the Resurrection of Christ (cf. 1:4; 4:25; 5:10; 6:9). The full reason for this only becomes clear when the next half of the verse is read; the line of thought moves from the realm of man's spirit to that of his body. *If Christ be in you,* there is life now in man's regenerate spirit. *If the Spirit of him that raised up Jesus from the dead dwell in you,* there will be life in the resurrection body. The phrase may be compared with the text in another paragraph: "Christ was raised from the dead through the glory of the Father" (6:4 R.V.). The name *Jesus* is used in this verse for the sake of its personal emphasis on His humanity: He is seen as the man who was put to death and laid in the grave. The God of peace brought Him back from the dead (Heb. 13:20), and His Spirit now dwells *in you.* We can only measure "the exceeding greatness of His power to us-ward" by a direct comparison with "the mighty power" which was brought into action to raise Him from the dead (Ephes. 1:19–20). If His Spirit now dwells in man, that man has an "earnest", a pledge, which is meant to assure him that mortality shall be swallowed up in newness of life (2 Cor. 5:5).

St. Paul's thought climbs to its full height in the last words which show that the promise of life is for body as well as for spirit: *he that raised up Christ Jesus from the dead shall quicken also*

[1] H. C. G. Moule: *Romans* (The Cambridge Bible), p. 145.
[2] εἰ δέ.

your mortal bodies through his Spirit that dwelleth in you (R.V.).
He whose Spirit now dwells in you shall quicken your mortal
bodies by that same indwelling Spirit; for the same power that
raised Christ from the dead shall raise you from the dead. The
name *Jesus* is amplified as *Christ Jesus,* because this points to
Him as the risen Saviour who has become the head of God's
redeemed people, and His Resurrection is viewed as a vital
nexus with theirs (cf. 1 Thess. 4:14; 1 Cor. 15:20). There is a
change from the word *raised up*[1] to the word *quicken;*[2] it means
to make alive (cf. 1 Cor. 15:22). This is more than restoration;
it points to the organic connection of the present with the
future, and it means to communicate that life of which He is
Lord and Author. This is only achieved *through his Spirit* or
because of his Spirit who dwells within: manuscript evidence
slightly favours the first rather than the second reading (cf.
2 Tim. 1:14). An incentive for holiness was put forward by
St. Paul in his claim that the body is "the temple of the Holy
Ghost which is in you" (1 Cor. 6:19); that incentive is
magnified in this verse which suggests that the body as the
temple in which He dwells is now an heir to "the hope of
glory" (Col. 1:27).

So this remarkable passage conducts our thought to the
final triumph of God's work on behalf of those who have the
mind of the Spirit: they have life now in their regenerate
spirit; they will enjoy life for ever in their resurrection body.
That frail mortal body must pass through the gate of death
or transformation, but it will at length be reunited with the
regenerate spirit to make up an undivided, wholly redeemed,
personality. Nicholas Count Von Zinzendorf gave the Moravian Brethren on his estate at Herrnhut the beautiful tradition
of an Easter service in God's Acre. The Brethren met before
daylight in the midst of their dead, waiting for the golden rim
of the sun to touch the sky with its Easter glory. Then the

[1] ὁ ἐγείρας.   [2] ζωοποιήσει.

words rang out: "The Lord is risen." And back came the shout in reply: "He is risen indeed." And their trombones woke the morning echoes as they led the anthem of praise, looking on to that great day when the dead in Christ will rise again.[1] Such a custom, simple enough, naïve perhaps, caught the very spirit of St. Paul's words; words of glorious rhetoric based on solid reason and culminating in mighty triumph. If dead men do not rise again, then Christ was not raised from the dead. And if Christ did not rise, their faith was in vain. And if their faith were all in vain, they were still in their sins. And if they were still in their sins, they were of all men most miserable. "But now is Christ risen from the dead, and become the firstfruits of them that slept . . . For as in Adam all die, even so in Christ shall all be made alive" (1 Cor. 15:20,22).

[1] J. E. Hutton: *A Short History of the Moravian Church*, p. 139.

CHAPTER SIX

We are Debtors

"Therefore, brethren, we are debtors, not to the flesh, to live after the flesh. For if ye live after the flesh, ye shall die: but if ye through the Spirit do mortify the deeds of the body, ye shall live." (A.V.)

"So then, brethren, we are debtors, not to the flesh, to live after the flesh: for if ye live after the flesh, ye must die; but if by the spirit ye mortify the deeds of the body, ye shall live." (R.V.)

"So then, brethren, we are debtors, not to the flesh, to live according to the flesh—for if you live according to the flesh you will die, but if by the Spirit you put to death the deeds of the body you will live." (R.S.V.)
— Romans 8:12–13

These two verses are the final pendant in the contrast between the mind of the flesh and the mind of the Spirit, and the first word *therefore, so then* (R.V.),[1] shows that they are meant to sum up the whole previous discussion. St. Paul employs a bold image in his choice of the word *debtors,* and he accords it an emphatic prominence in the structure of the sentence. Men are seldom willing to own up to their debts; they would rather be thought of as benefactors than as debtors. But St. Paul found the most compelling interest in the idea that he was a debtor to God, and it formed one of the driving motives in his approach

[1] ἄρα οὖν.

to life. He had been a debtor in the necessity for forgiveness and acceptance with God. He had less than nothing with which to pay what he knew that he owed, and he could do no more than ask God to forgive all that was due (cf. Matt. 6:12). It was because he had nothing in hand that God "frankly forgave" him all that debt (Luke 7:42). Now he was a debtor in the necessity for holiness and fellowship with God. He knew that his release from the burden of sin imposed on him a new obligation for a life of continual obedience; what would he say? Would he say that it was admirable as an ideal, but impossible in practice? Not now; for he was a debtor, and he had Christ within, and this meant that all the riches of His grace were available to meet that debt. This is comparable with his declaration in the preface of this letter: "I am debtor both to the Greeks, and to the Barbarians; both to the wise, and to the unwise. So, as much as in me is, I am ready to preach the gospel" (1:14,15). It was not a question of choice or charity whether he should preach the Gospel; it was a sense of debt and duty by which he was impelled. So too we are under obligation to live up to the full height of our new spiritual status as those who have been made free from the law of sin and death.

The text begins with a negative reference to the mind of the flesh: *therefore, brethren, we are debtors, not to the flesh, to live after the flesh*. St. Paul identified himself with his readers by his use of the word *brethren* and by his return to the first person plural (cf. 8:4). As for the flesh, he said, we owe nothing at all in that quarter; God has condemned sin in the flesh of His own Son so that we should not live on that level. He had referred in the last verse to the divine purpose for the body viewed as something distinct from the flesh: it will be quickened by means of His Spirit who dwells within (cf. 8:11). But that glorious destiny has its obligations in the present as well as its promise for the future, and makes it all the more imperative that we should "make no provision for the flesh to fulfil the lusts thereof (13:14). The flesh is a false and ruinous creditor; its claims are all stamped with fraud and deceit: but we owe it nothing except to nail it to the Cross (Gal. 5:24).

This verse is an interesting illustration of a trick of rhetoric known as meiosis where less is said than is implied, and the meaning can be brought out if we add the words which would round off the sentence: *but to the Spirit, to live after the Spirit.* St. Paul broke off before the sentence was finished, knowing that the meaning was plain. The truth is that, so far are we from all debt to the flesh, that the very reverse is now the case; we are instead debtors to the Spirit. This thought buries its roots in the earlier discussion and draws its strength from the sober logic of the context. It is because Christ is in us that our regenerate spirit is now alive (8:10); and our regenerate spirit owes its life to the life-giving Spirit of God who is in us just as Christ is in us (8:11). Therefore our true obligation now lies towards the Lord and Life-giver without whom we would still be in bondage to sin and death. That debt to Him is not a black burden; it is a thing of joy: for "now we owe, and we have Christ in us" to pay all that is due.[1]

The next words turn back to direct address in the second person and are a fresh affirmation that the way of the flesh results in death: *for if ye live after the flesh, ye shall die.* This points to the law of cause and effect; the one must lead to the other. Therefore to live on the level of the flesh means that *ye must die* (R.V.); there can be no escape, "for the end of those things is death" (6:21). The flesh, like sin, is a sure pay-master; it may not pay at the end of each day, or each month, or each year; but it always pays in the end, and its wages are death (6:23). Such a term is comprehensive; it means death as the full penal judgment on sin. It is death in body and in spirit, both now and for ever. No one who reads St. Paul's terrible

[1] H. C. G. Moule: *Romans* (The Expositor's Bible), p. 220.

catalogue of the works of the flesh will be surprised at his verdict that "they which do such things shall not inherit the kingdom of God" (Gal. 5:21). He could not have been more drastic in his words of warning: "Be not deceived; God is not mocked; for whatsoever a man soweth, that shall he also reap; for he that soweth to his flesh shall of the flesh reap corruption" (Gal. 6:7-8).

The text concludes with a positive reference to the mind of the Spirit: *but if ye through the Spirit do mortify the deeds of the body, ye shall live.* These words are in antithesis to the last words and show that the necessity for holiness is absolute: for men must die unless through the Spirit they put to death the deeds of the body. The word *mortify* seems to have been suggested by the phrase *ye shall die.* It is as stern and strong as a figure of speech can be; it means to do a thing to death, to make it die, slow and painful as that process may prove. "Mortify therefore your members which are upon the earth" (Col. 3:5). We are never exempt from the elements and conditions of evil in "the body of sin" (6:6), and can never dispense with the Holy Spirit as the mighty "counter-agent" to its doings.[1] The term *body* does not mean quite the same thing as the term *flesh*; it is used here in the way of metonymy, as the grammarians call it. The part stands for the whole; the deeds performed in the body as the organ of sin mean the sinful doings of the whole man.[2] To put these things to death is the secret of life indeed.

These two verses confront us with the same alternatives as does verse six: "The mind of the flesh is death, but the mind of the Spirit is life and peace" (R.V.). The requirements for holiness do not consist in a formula or a discipline; they call for the constant process of resistance and denial by means of the Holy Spirit who dwells within. Dr. John MacBeath has pointed out that the mind of the flesh may express itself through

---

[1] H. C. G. Moule: *Romans* (The Expositor's Bible), p. 221.
[2] Charles Hodge: op. cit., p. 263.

the sweetest things or moments in life. "In that picture of Saint Bartholomew's Eve, painted by Millais, the young Huguenot's temptation came from the very lips and eyes of the girl he loved. Love to her was everything; to him, love had another allegiance. He had a certain loyalty towards her, but there was another loyalty, stronger and keener, so that when she tied around his arm the white kerchief, the badge of the Catholics, as his defence against the threatened slaughter of the morrow—even as he clasped her, he unfastened with firm fingers the knot that her hands had tied. And as he in his quiet gentle strength looked down into her eyes, she grew strong in his strength." Then Dr. MacBeath went on to say that this is the only thing which can save us from life's perilous unguardedness: it is the sense of a higher loyalty. "Temptation comes ever so swiftly, but Christ comes as swiftly too."[1] And if through His Holy Spirit as the mighty "counter-agent" within[2] we put to death the deeds of "the body of sin" (6:6), verily, we shall live.

[1] Dr. John MacBeath: The Keswick Convention (1935), p. 137.
[2] H. C. G. Moule: op. cit., p. 221.

CHAPTER SEVEN

The Sons of God

"For as many as are led by the Spirit of God, they are the sons of God." (A.V.)

"For as many as are led by the Spirit of God, these are sons of God." (R.V.)

"For all who are led by the Spirit of God are sons of God." (R.S.V.)

—Romans 8:14

This verse stands at the head of a new line of thought in which the work of the Holy Spirit holds the place of paramount interest (8:14–27). The first word *for* is the necessary link with the whole previous paragraph and points back to the last clause in particular. There are instructive parallels in the structure of these verses and the movement of thought is clear. The one change is that the pronoun alters back to the third person for the new and definitive sentence, and a paraphrase will set out the argument in its fundamental simplicity: if you through the Spirit put sin to death, then you will live; and you will live because all who are led by the Spirit of God are sons of God. St. Paul's former exhortation to "*walk* after the Spirit" (8:4) is almost identical with the current definition of those who are now "*led* by the Spirit". But his thought moves forward as well, for he now turns from the concept of *life* to that of *sons*. Both are linked with the work of the Holy Spirit, but a deeper level is plumbed; the gift of *life* is seen as the proof of *sonship*, and such sonship goes to the heart of God Himself.

The two leading ideas of God's Spirit and man's sonship are then interwoven in a remarkable pattern: *for as many as are led by the Spirit of God, they are the sons of God.* The qualities of emphasis are spread with an equal balance between each clause; this is in fact so much the case that they can be reversed without change of meaning. Only those who are led by the Spirit are sons of God; and the sons of God are always those who are led by the Spirit. This sharpness of statement belongs to the very essence of Pauline dogma and definition; it has the great merit of precision and clarity in the affirmation of truth.

The first clause points upward to the Holy Spirit by whom men must be led: *for as many as are led by the Spirit of God.* A clear illustration of what this means is found in the Lucan record of our Lord's life: "Jesus, being full of the Holy Ghost, returned from Jordan, and was *led by the Spirit* into the wilderness" (Luke 4:1). St. Luke refers to two distinct aspects of His relationship to the Holy Spirit, and each must be kept in proper focus: it is only one who is filled with the Spirit who can be led by the Spirit. There is nothing here to impair man's own intrinsic character as an individual personality; the thing that is in view is that searching, penetrative, personal influence of the Spirit of God in the inmost region of man's being. This means that man is called upon to yield the "springs of thought and will" to His control;[1] he must welcome His rule in the great keep of the City of Mansoul. This is to let Him rule and regulate the whole realm of mind and feeling; then, as that man responds and obeys, he will be led by the Spirit. This does not point to some unreal fancy or some irrational impulse; it is something which has its seat in the hidden laboratories of a man's soul where the Holy Spirit moves and impels one who is led by Him.

This clause may be compared with St. Paul's words in a

[1] H. C. G. Moule: op. cit., p. 223.

similar paragraph in which he had explained that all those
who belong to Christ must put to death the flesh with its
lusts and desires: "If we live in the Spirit, let us also walk in the
Spirit" (Gal. 5:25). Those who are led by the Spirit and those
who walk in the Spirit are the self-same people, and the context
in each case makes it clear that this ought to be the daily
pattern of their life and conduct. St. Paul did not limit it to
some high moment of elation or emotion; it is not an experience
which is governed by mysticism or enthusiasm. It is as down to
earth as to be led by the hand or to walk in the way would
imply; it means obedience to the rule of God's will in mind,
mouth, and manhood. There need never be an hour in which
this is not true in the life of one who has been made free from
the law of sin and death. It should be the normal experience
of all who are doing to death the deeds of the body by means of
the Spirit who dwells within.

The next clause points inward to the divine sonship by which
men should be known: *they are the sons of God*. This term[1] is all
the more remarkable when we remind ourselves that God's only
Son in the most rigid meaning of that term[2] is Jesus, Emmanuel,
both Lord and Christ; yet God's purpose when He sent Him
into the world was that He should be "the firstborn among
many brethren" (8:29). Therefore to be reckoned as *the sons of
God* means recognition by the Father that we belong to the
"many brethren" of Him who is called the "firstborn". "For ye
are all *sons*[1] of God, through faith, in Christ Jesus" (Gal.
3:26 R.V.). "Ye shall be my *sons*[1] and daughters, saith the
Lord Almighty" (2 Cor. 6:18). This is infinitely more than to
stand in the place of creatures in the presence of their Maker; it
is more, far more, than to stand in the place of servants in the
presence of their Master. It means that such a man has a new
and vital status in the divine household; he now belongs to it
as one who is a son of God. He may be called other names in

---

[1] *vioi.*   [2] See John 3:16; Romans 8:32; *viós.*

other circumstances; he may be known as a disciple or a believer. But such names are incidental to the ultimate reality: he is a son, dearer and more welcome to the Father's heart and in the Father's presence than he can know.[1]

This clause may be compared with St. Paul's words in a similar paragraph in which he had referred to the conflict between the flesh and the Spirit. "If ye be led of the Spirit, ye are not under the law" (Gal. 5:18). We were bondmen under the law, but now we are the sons of God; and there is a striking contrast between the old state of bondage and this new and active life of freedom. We are not slaves who toil and sweat beneath the lash of law; we are not servants; we are not strangers; we are the sons of God, at home in the Father's household. There was a time when we might have been glad to be known as one of the "hired servants" (Luke 15:19); but the time has now come when we hear the Father Himself declare: "Son, thou art ever with me, and all that I have is thine" (Luke 15:31). This idea of sonship has a threefold implication. It means that we bear the Father's name and reflect His character, and we are put in trust with all that such a name implies: "That ye may be *sons*[2] of your Father which is in heaven" (Matt. 5:45, R.V.). It means that we know the Father's love and enjoy His affection, and that love is now shed abroad within our hearts by means of His Spirit: "Behold what manner of love the Father hath bestowed upon us, that we should be called children of God" (1 John 3:1, R.V.). It means that we share the Father's home and receive its benefits, and we delight in the dignity and the privilege which it confers: "There shall they be called *sons*[3] of the living God" (Rom. 9:26, R.V.). Those who are led of the Spirit are no more like bondmen "under the law" (Gal. 5:18); they have entered into all the "glorious liberty of the children of God" (8:21).

[1] See H. C. G. Moule: op. cit., p. 224.   [2] *viol.*   [3] *viol.*

Such a verse is like a ladder which has been set up from earth to heaven, and its lowest rungs are within the reach of all: *for as many as are led by the Spirit of God, they are the sons of God.* The most faltering believer only needs to look with habitual simplicity to the Spirit of God to light and lead him in the way, and he may then rejoice in the knowledge that he belongs to the Father's household. Why is it then that so many fail to grasp their calling as sons of God and are strangers to that "glorious liberty" (8:21)? This is no close-guarded secret from which any are meant to be shut out; it is not something which God seeks to reserve only for the few. He has no favourites and does not circumscribe His love; all who are led by the Spirit of God are meant to share all that divine sonship entails. "All things are yours, whether . . . the world, or life, or death, or things present, or things to come; . . . and ye are Christ's; and Christ is God's" (1 Cor. 3:21–23). Perhaps Augustus Toplady's "Hymn To The Blessed Spirit"[1] may voice our prayer:

> "Holy Ghost, dispel our sadness;
> Pierce the clouds of sinful night:
> Come, Thou source of sweetest gladness;
> Breathe Thy life and spread Thy light."

[1] Augustus Toplady: *Complete Works*, p. 910.

CHAPTER EIGHT

Abba, Father

"For ye have not received the Spirit of bondage again to fear: but ye have received the Spirit of adoption, whereby we cry, Abba, Father." (A.V.)

"For ye received not the spirit of bondage again unto fear; but ye received the spirit of adoption, whereby we cry, Abba, Father." (R.V.)

"For you did not receive the spirit of slavery to fall back into fear, but you have received the spirit of sonship. When we cry, 'Abba! Father!' . . ." (R.S.V.)

—Romans 8:15

This verse refers to the Holy Spirit as the Author of our new nature and its true feelings, and His work is described by means of a striking contrast: *for ye have not received the Spirit of bondage again to fear, but ye have received the Spirit of adoption whereby we cry, Abba, Father.* The first word *for* provides the link with the last verse. St. Paul had just identified those who are led by the Spirit as the sons of God, and this led on to the contrast between the anxieties of bondage and the benefits of adoption. It is often argued that the phrase *"the Spirit of bondage"* involves no more than a subtle variation in the use of the word *spirit,* and means such a spirit as would characterise the lot of slaves.[1] The phrase in fact could have been used in this sense as when he spoke of "the spirit of meekness" (1 Cor. 4:21) or

[1] See A. V.; R.V.; R.S.V.

"the spirit of fear" (2 Tim. 1:7). But the context is in favour of a personal reference to the Holy Spirit, and this becomes certain in the further concept of *the Spirit of adoption* (cf. Gal. 4:6): He who had been spoken of as "in you" (8:11) is here represented as the Author of the feelings of those in whom He dwells. The fact that the verbs are in the aorist tense points to a distinct crisis in past experience and the meaning may be clarified by a paraphrase: for the Holy Spirit whom you received does not cause a relapse into the old state of slavish anxiety such as you felt while you were still under the law; He floods your heart with the filial attitudes of trust and love which will constrain you to join in the cry, Abba, Father. There is a close affinity between this great saying and the dictum that now in Christ Jesus, "the law of the Spirit of life" makes men free from "the law of sin and death" (8:2).

The first part of this text states the case in terms of negative emphasis: *for ye (did) not receive the Spirit of bondage again to fear.* What is meant by the reference to *bondage?* It can only refer back to the state of all who are under the law; it "gendereth to bondage" (Gal. 4:24). The man who puts his trust in the works of the law must live and toil like a slave at the beck and call of a master tyrant. This is true of all who have the mind of the flesh, whether they are aware of it or not; they serve what is in fact "the law of sin and death" (8:2). They are secret rebels against the law which must command; they are sullen bondmen under the law which must subdue. Conscience will not always allow men to live as though there were no divine authority but its operations produce little more than passing efforts to respond and obey. All such efforts are reluctant and tentative with the result that they remain "through fear of death . . . all their lifetime subject to bondage" (Heb. 2:15). This is the state of all who wear the yoke of law; it is that state of mind in which men shrink from God as a master who would bind them against their will.[1]

[1] H. C. G. Moule: op. cit., 223.

All such bondage leads of necessity to *fear,* and such fear has torment. The slaves of law live in constant apprehension of the righteous judgment of God, for they know that inadequate obedience can only result in final condemnation. The scant service which they try to render finds its only motive in the craven fear of what all failure deserves, and each fresh breach of the law is bound to increase their deep inner anxiety in view of the judgment to come. It may be true that men often live long lives in apparent unconcern for "things of the Spirit" (8:5); years may pass by while they resist the claims of law and the pressure of guilt. They do not see themselves as slaves, and there is no fear of God in their minds. But sooner or later, in the crises of life or the issues of death, they reach a point where there is no further escape. Then their state of mind is one of nervous alarm because they see at last that there is no way out of that bondage to sin and death.

St. Paul applied these facts to his readers: they had not received the Spirit of life as the Author of those fears which belong to servitude. The word *again* clearly alludes to their harassed state of feeling before they had received the mind of the Spirit. It would recall the bleak monotony of life when they had been under the law and its bondage, when they had thought of God only as a judge whom they had defied. But now, in Christ Jesus, the law of the Spirit of life had made them free, and it was no function of that Spirit to drag them back into bondage and fear. Their real freedom was all the more strongly affirmed by means of this negative assertion. When God gave and when they received that Spirit of grace, what did He do for them: did He lead them back once more to the old state of sullen bondage and fear? St. Paul's deliberate reply was that the law of the Spirit of life had made them free; He was not the Author of bondage, and would never seek to reduce them to the dark anxieties of their old life under the law of sin and death.

The next part of this text states the case in terms of positive emphasis: *but ye (did) receive the Spirit of adoption whereby we cry, Abba, Father.* What is meant by the reference to *adoption*? It can only point to the state of all who are under the grace of God; it is the proof of that freedom "wherewith Christ hath made us free" (Gal. 5:1). The concept of freedom is the natural opposite to a state of bondage, but St. Paul reached for an even higher concept and chose a word that would convey the thought of our welcome as sons in the Father's household. The word *adoption*[1] was derived from a classical phrase,[2] and this points to the quarter from which St. Paul took the idea: it was Greek, not Hebrew.[3] The tradition of adoption was unknown in Jewish circles, but was common in the social life of both Greece and Rome. It meant that the status of sonship was conferred by law on one who was born of other parents. Such an adopted son was not in the least inferior to a son of the house: he was taken into that house to bear its name and to share its inheritance. The metaphor of adoption was used by St. Paul to show that "we are by grace what Christ is by nature";[4] we have been brought into a new, legal relationship with God, akin to, but distinct from, the unique sonship of Christ. "God sent forth His Son . . . to redeem them that were under the law, that we might receive the adoption of sons" (Gal. 4:4,5; cf. Ephes. 1:5).

If the ideas of bondage and freedom were in contrast, then the idea of fear may be seen as opposed to that of love; but his heart was enlarged, and he made the contrast in a phrase of even greater beauty. Just as he had reached up from the idea of freedom to the higher concept of sonship, so he reached up from the idea of love to the richer concept of those who cry *Abba, Father.* He turned once more to the use of the first person in his

[1] υἱοθεσίας. [2] υἱός τίθεσθαι.
[3] W. Sanday and A. C. Headlam: op. cit., p. 203.
[4] A. M. Hunter: op. cit., p. 80.

deep sense of the oneness of the divine household and spoke of their common access to God with the loving freedom with which children come to their father. It is almost as though he would remind them of the words: "When ye pray, say, Our Father which art in heaven" (Luke 11:2). The phrase *Abba, Father,* joins an Aramaic word with a Greek word in a way which must recall the fact that the Gospel had its birth in the midst of a bilingual people.[1] It is rare for any other than man's mother tongue to become interwoven with his inmost thoughts and feelings to such a point that it wells up in a spontaneous exclamation when the heart is overflowing; and expressions of tenderness are the last traits of one's mother language that man gives up.[2] The use of the definite article before the Greek word may show that it was meant to give the meaning of the Aramaic *Abba*; but such explanation seems out of place in such a *cri de cœur*. Repetition can be readily understood if the speaker were at home in both tongues; it would throb with greater intensity.[3] The phrase *Abba, Father,* had been used by the Lord Himself in an hour of darkest anguish, and it is one of the few words spoken in His mother tongue to have been preserved in the vernacular (see Mark 14:36). It had a strong emotional content and had almost become a name for God on the lips of St. Paul.[4] "God hath sent forth the Spirit of His Son into your hearts, crying, Abba, Father" (Gal. 4:6).

St. Paul applied these facts to his readers: for they had received the Spirit of life as the Author of the joys that belong to adoption. The words *we cry* clearly allude to this filial confidence which His presence within would now inspire. St. Paul implied that no bondman would address his master by a name so dear and tender; the use of such a name is the exclusive

---

[1] W. Sanday and A. C. Headlam: op. cit., p. 203.
[2] Charles Hodge: op. cit., p. 264.
[3] W. Sanday and A. C. Headlam: op. cit., p. 203.
[4] H. C. G. Moule: op. cit., p. 223 fn.

privilege of sons in the Father's household. And while they had once been strangers who had no rights in His presence, they were now nothing less than sons. The once trembling sinners, full of servile fear, could now lean on His arm in perfect quietness; and his Spirit, dwelling within, would prompt them to call Him *Abba, Father,* just as Jesus Himself had done. For now, in Christ Jesus, the law of the Spirit of life had made them free, and it was the function of that Spirit to call forth in them the feelings of true sonship. Their real freedom was all the more strongly affirmed by means of this positive assertion. When God gave and when they received that Spirit of grace, what did He do for them? Did He not treat them as sons who are now dearer than words can tell in the inmost circle of light and love?[1] St. Paul's deliberate reply was that God had sent His Spirit into their hearts and that He would lead them into His own presence with the password *Abba, Father.*

This verse has been the staff and stay of men in the darkest hours of distress. It was during 1869, at the age of thirty-seven, that James Hudson Taylor entered into a new spiritual experience which he described to his sister. It came at a time when he felt as though he were involved in a losing battle. He saw himself as a man who hated sin and yet he suffered defeat; he was struggling against it, but he was close to despair. But there was one ray of light and comfort, even before he found all that God had in store for him, and he described it in words that are still memorable: "I felt I was a child of God: His Spirit in my heart would cry, in spite of all, Abba, Father."[2] This was scarcely less true in the case of John Donne, the poet and preacher, who had become the Dean of St. Paul's in 1621. His once mordant wit was channelled into new ways of thought as the result of a decisive conversion, and all the gifts of his early

[1] H. C. G. Moule: op. cit., p. 223.
[2] Dr. and Mrs. Howard Taylor: *Hudson Taylor and The China Inland Mission,* p. 174.

poems were brought to bear in his Hymn to God the Father in
which he made clear all the fears and hopes of his own soul:[1]

"Wilt Thou forgive that sin where I begun,
    Which was my sin, though it were done before?
Wilt Thou forgive that sin through which I run,
    And do run still, though still I do deplore?
When Thou hast done, Thou hast not done;
    For I have more.

"I have a sin of fear, that when I've spun
    My last thread, I shall perish on the shore;
But swear by Thyself that at my death Thy Son
    Shall shine as He shines now and heretofore:
And having done that, Thou hast done;
    I fear no more."

[1] *The Oxford Book of English Verse 1250–1900*, pp. 230–1.

CHAPTER NINE

The Joint Witness

"The Spirit itself beareth witness with our spirit, that we are the children of God." (A.V.)

"The Spirit himself beareth witness with our spirit, that we are children of God." (R.V.)

"It is the Spirit himself bearing witness with our spirit that we are children of God." (R.S.V.)

—Romans 8:16

This text grows out of the last verse and stands in such intimate connection with it that the R.S.V. makes it read: "When we cry, 'Abba! Father!' it is the Spirit himself bearing witness with our spirit that we are the children of God." The true office and ministry of *the Spirit of adoption* is seen in that cry of filial reverence: He moves and prompts our heart to cry *Abba, Father,* and when it cries like that, He bears witness with our spirit that we are the children of God. The verb *beareth witness*[1] must be given the full meaning of its compound form, for it points to two distinct sources of this testimony. This is clear from its use in two other verses in which the joint witness was the subjective testimony of conscience and the objective testimony of action (2:15; 9:1). In the case of this verse St. Paul sought to analyse a man's sense of awareness, and he ascribed all his conscious feelings in part to the Holy Spirit who dwells within and in part to the man himself as a living, regenerate,

[1] συνμαρτυρεῖ.

human unit.[1] As a result, he spoke of the inner voices, the voice
of the Holy Spirit and the voice of man's own regenerate
spirit, whose joint witness assures him that he is a child of God.
The word which the Holy Spirit prompts and which our
spirit cries is *Abba, Father,* and the witness of His presence
concurs with the witness of our feelings to prove that we are
His children. There is a slight emphasis in the position of
the word *are* and there is a change from the word *sons*[2] to the
word *children*.[3] St. Paul spoke of *sons* and *children* in terms
which make it hard to draw any absolute distinction; but if
there were any subtle nuance at all in the change from *sons* to
children, it would only add to the strength of this statement.
Sons may enter a family by adoption; children are born into
the home: and God by His Spirit now bears witness with our
spirit that we are both sons and children.

St. Paul begins with an explicit reference to the witness of
God's Holy Spirit to the fact that we are members of the divine
household: *the Spirit himself beareth witness with our spirit, that
we are the children of God.* St. Paul was not concerned with the
psychic experience of men who claim that they have seen
visions or heard voices. Such things may take place now and
then as he knew from his own experience (2 Cor. 12:1–4);
but they become suspect once they depart from the laws of
strict economy, and then they can only be thought of as false
and illusory. But there is such a thing as an express revelation of
the grace and goodness of God: "He that believeth on the Son
of God hath the witness in himself" (1 John 5:10). It is as
though there were a voice, unheard by the outward ear, yet
perfectly audible in the inmost region of the spirit, that lets a
man know that he is the child of God. Such a distinctive
utterance in the soul of that man is an infallible witness to the
love that God has for him, and that witness is a direct result

[1] W. Sanday and A. C. Headlam: op. cit., p. 203.
[2] *υἱοί.*   [3] *τέκνα.*

of the unseen presence of the Holy Spirit who takes the things of Christ and shows them to the heart (John 16:15). It may be as hard to express in words how this is done as it is to explain how yet other effects of His presence can be produced in heart and mind. But we need not deny what we cannot explain, "because the love of God is shed abroad in our hearts by the Holy Ghost which is given unto us" (5:5). And this He does in ways of His own to assure the heart of the love which God has for His children.

The chief way in which His Spirit bears this witness is found in the facts of His Word: He brings home to the once cold and unresponsive heart the sober reality of its message of grace and love. Man stands in need of a direct and a particular saying of God to his inmost spirit such as David longed to receive: "Say unto my soul, I am thy salvation" (Ps. 35;3). But the written Word of God will only prove the living voice of God when it is read or heard in the power of the Holy Spirit. Then He will bring home some divine promise with such fresh and vivid meaning that there is no escape (e.g. John 6:37; Rev. 3:20). One may often have heard the self-same words before, and yet have failed to take them in. But now, as the Word of God falls on the ear and the voice of God speaks to the heart, he finds himself gladly aware that the Gospel is in fact true for him. So it was in the case of John Bunyan when the text of Scripture (Heb. 12:22–24) shone with reality for him. "And then", he cried, "with joy I told my wife, O now I know, I know. That night was a good night to me; I never had but few better."[1] It is not what man may feel that matters; it is what God has said that counts. Man's feelings are always changing, but God's Word does not change. That Word stands for ever, and its invitations mean what they say. All that remains for man is to take God at His Word and

[1] Grace Abounding to The Chief of Sinners (see the *Works of John Bunyan*, edited by George Offor, vol. 1, p. 40).

to rest by faith on His promise. If such a man be asked how he knows that he is a child of God, he can truly reply that he has the witness of God's Spirit through the facts of His Word.

St. Paul proceeds with an implicit reference to the witness of our regenerate human spirit to the fact that we are members of the divine household: *the Spirit himself beareth witness with our spirit that we are the children of God*. St. Paul's words make it clear that God's Holy Spirit not only bears witness to our spirit; He also bears witness *with* our spirit. This must imply that our spirit has its work of testimony no less than His Spirit, and the value of this testimony is just as real even though it may be subordinate. The man in whose heart the love of God has been shed abroad becomes humbly aware that he loves in return. That man begins with a discovery which transcends all ordinary comprehension: "Herein is love, not that we loved God, but that he loved us, and sent his Son to be the propitiation for our sins" (1 John 4:10). And that discovery evokes a response which transforms all ordinary experience: "We love him, because he first loved us" (1 John 4:19). This means that God's Holy Spirit meets and concurs with man's regenerate spirit in a common testimony to the fact that he is a child of God. It means that the witness of our spirit is upheld and confirmed by the witness of His Spirit so that the truth is owned and made clear on both sides. The two distinct lines of witness unite to form the same strong and happy verdict that He is our Father and we are His children. The love of God is known and felt beyond all doubt as His Holy Spirit keeps tryst with our spirit, and we are moved in the inmost region of our being to voice the cry, *Abba, Father.*

The chief way in which our spirit bears this witness is found in the marks of His grace: it brings home to the once dark and apprehensive heart the solid reality of God's action of grace and love. "As many as received him, to them gave he power to become the sons of God, even to them that believe

E

on his name" (John 1:12). Such an experience involves a change of heart which cannot be denied: old things must pass away, and all things are made new. The marks of grace must make themselves clear in Christian character; they must provide the proof that a man is now a member of the household of God. There is new love, a love for Christ as the mighty Saviour which was not known before; and none love Him like that unless they are children of God. There is new peace, a peace with God as the gracious Father which was not known before; and none have peace like that unless they are children of God. So it was in the case of the Cornish miner, Billy Bray, who could not repress his joy. "I can't help praising the Lord", he said. "As I go along the street, I lift up one foot, and it seems to say *Glory*. And I lift up the other, and it seems to say *Amen*. And so they keep on like that all the time I am walking."[1] No two men will ever have just the same experience when grace begins to work: the details will differ as men themselves differ. But the result will be the same in the case of every authentic conversion, and no one can mistake the change which this involves. The marks of grace may at times be clear and distinct in the eyes of others while they are yet dark and obscure in the eyes of the man himself. But the time may come when God will so shine on them that he cannot remain in doubt. If such a man be asked how he knows that he is a child of God, he can truly reply that he has the witness of a regenerate spirit through the marks of His grace.

There are thus two distinct lines of witness in the experience of God's children. They may not both disclose themselves at the same time in the experience of some particular person, but they are both integral elements of true Christian assurance. It is always easy to have clearer understanding about them than direct experience of them, and it is rash for a man to rely on one rather than the other or to ignore one for the sake of the other.

[1] F. W. Bourne: *Billy Bray*, p. 43.

But when that man becomes aware of the concurrent evidence of both, he can apply this verse to his own case with full personal assurance: "The Spirit himself beareth witness *with my spirit* that I am a child of God." It is true that a man may be a child of God, and yet lack this authentic assurance; he may have "the Spirit of Christ" (8:9), and yet tremble to cry "Abba, Father" (8:15). Such were Bunyan's *dramatis personæ*, Mr. Fearing, Much-Afraid, and others, in *The Pilgrim's Progress*. They were received at last within the gates of the city, but their journey thither was full of doubt and fear. This] is no state in which to live, still less in which to die; and why should a man be content with the twilight of such spiritual uncertainty? God has better plans for all His children than that; He would not wish any child of His to remain in doubt that He is their Father. If a man is not sure, he would be wise never to rest until he can say from his heart that now he knows. St. Paul had no shadow of fear or doubt; he could cry with glorious certainty: "I know whom I have believed, and am persuaded that he is able to keep that which I have committed unto him against that day" (2 Tim. 1:12). No man should be content until that same glorious certainty is his as well.

CHAPTER TEN

Joint-heirs with Christ

"And if children, then heirs; heirs of God, and joint-heirs with Christ; if so be that we suffer with him, that we may be also glorified together." (A.V.)

"And if children, then heirs; heirs of God, and joint-heirs with Christ; if so be that we suffer with him, that we may be also glorified with him." (R.V.)

"And if children, then heirs, heirs of God and fellow heirs with Christ, provided we suffer with him in order that we may also be glorified with him." (R.S.V.)

—Romans 8:17

There is continuous upward movement in this passage as its thought climbs from step to step like the ascent of a stairway. The work of the Spirit does not exhaust itself in the divine witness with our spirit that we are God's children, for part of this testimony is to show that sonship leads to heirship and all that such heirship implies: *and if children, then heirs; heirs of God, and joint-heirs with Christ; if so be that we suffer with him, that we may be also glorified together.* There is not the least pause in the sequence of thought as it moves from a place in the divine household as sons straight to a share in the divine patrimony as heirs; we are in fact joint-heirs with Christ, partners with the firstborn. This has repercussions in the present just as real as in the future; it means that we are called upon to share in His travail before we share in His glory. St. Paul's purpose was to focus our eyes on the hope of glory towards which the whole argument now began to gravitate, and he viewed it as an inheritance which is entailed on all who are children of God. Such an inheritance stands quite apart from all idea of work and wage; it has nothing to do with fees and dues. It is a gift which men neither earn nor deserve, but which they are yet to receive under the will of the divine benefactor. The idea of inheritance was a favourite element in Old Testament law and history, but the immediate background for the image in this context was the practice in the Roman law-courts. What was owned by inheritance was even more secure than what might be owned by purchase, and the ordinary inheritance of the first-born was as nothing compared with the promised inheritance of God's children (Heb. 9:15). Nothing can deprive the members of His household of that glorious heritage now in prospect, for it is the lawful portion of all who are lawful children.[1]

St. Paul's first words assert the facts of this inheritance with a laconic dignity: *and if children, then heirs; heirs of God, and joint-heirs with Christ*. The metaphor of adoption is the guiding factor for a correct exegesis of this statement since it was based on the realities of this custom in the law and society of Rome. The head of a household was allowed to adopt the son of a stranger by means of a legal ceremony. Several witnesses were required to attend so that there could be no doubt with regard to what was done. It involved the fiction of a sale and purchase in which rights were conveyed from house to house, and the utterance of a formula for the public acknowledgment of the adopted son on the part of the adoptive father. A pair of scales was then struck with a wand of brass as a sign that the legal transfer was deemed complete. That ceremony would confer the status of sonship on the person concerned with a finality

[1] H. C. G. Moule: op. cit., p. 225.

that was beyond dispute. Such a son by law came into the home and clan as though he were a son by birth. He took its name and shared its rights in a way that put an end to the ties of his old life. It wiped out all his debts and was as strong a bar to all intermarriage within the house as blood relationship itself. That son outranked certain other members of the household and was secured in his rights of inheritance.[1] And this was so well known that St. Paul could borrow the whole field of thought to explain to his Gentile converts what their status was as the sons of God. They could now cry Abba, Father; and if any should call this right into question, they could rely on a divine witness who would declare them to be His children. This would imply not only the cancellation of debts, but the hope of glory as well; for if they were children, then they were heirs. "Thou art no more a servant, but a son; and if a son, then an heir of God through Christ" (Gal. 4:7).

St. Paul expounds this right to share in the divine inheritance in terms of a joint and equal heirship with Christ. This is one of the most daring of all Pauline concepts and was derived from the complex law of Roman inheritance. It was meant to eliminate the fact of death and to stress the absolute unity between the head of the household and his heir or group of co-heirs: he lived on as it were in them and was in law the same person with them. Such an idea imbues St. Paul's language with a meaning and a congruity that are sublime: God lives as it were in His heirs, and they are all fellow-heirs with His Son.[2] God treats all His children as heirs, and there is no priority of order or favour among those who share this inheritance. Nor is this all; they are joint-heirs with Christ Himself. He had described Himself as "the heir" in the course of His parable on the husbandmen (Matt. 21:38), and the idea of a divine inheritance received its true adaptation from Him

[1] W. E. Ball: *St. Paul and The Roman Law*, pp. 4–8.
[2] Ibid., pp. 13–17.

(Matt. 25:34).[1] He has been named as the "heir of all things" (Heb. 1:2), and He invites all His brethren to share in His inheritance. To be joint-heirs with Him means that they will receive as a matter of grace all that is His as a matter of right. Thus it was for *the joy* in store that He endured the Cross (Heb. 12:2), and all who tread in His footsteps will hear Him say: "Enter thou into *the joy* of thy Lord" (Matt. 25:21). The sons of God do not all in this life enjoy the same gifts or possess the same material blessings: they are not all rich or influential; they are not all strong or useful. But they are all joint-heirs with Christ, and what more can adopted children wish for than to inherit as much as the firstborn? And the secret lies in that one word *if:* "And *if* children, then heirs", and all that such heir-ship with Christ implies.

St. Paul's next words assert the rules of this inheritance with a dogmatic certainty: *if so be that we suffer with him, that we may be also glorified together.* All that belongs to Christ as the first-born belongs to His brethren as well, and this includes a dark side as well as a bright. It was necessary for Him first to suffer, and only then to enter into His glory (Luke 24:26; Acts 17:3); and what was true in His experience is the pattern to which ours will conform. We are joint-heirs *if so be that,* provided that or on condition that, we are willing to share the cross before we hope to wear the crown. God had only one Son who was without sin, and none at all who is not called to suffer; for all suffering has its genesis in sin, and no one is immune from the pains of a world gone wrong. But of all the many thousands who are at one given moment subject to grief and pain, how few can be described as those who are called to suffer with Him? This verse does not speak of universal forms of sorrow, but pains that are due to our union with Him.[2] It is quite true that His vicarious sorrows were endured for others and cannot be

---

[1] W. Sanday and A. C. Headlam: op. cit., p. 204.
[2] H. C. G. Moule: op. cit., p. 225.

transferred in part or whole; yet how can we escape sorrow if we take up our cross and tread in the footsteps of the man of sorrows? There is a sense in which we may learn to know Him in the fellowship of His sufferings (Phil. 3:10); we may fill up that which remains of the afflictions of our Redeemer (Col. 1:24). We are called to drink of the cup of which He drank and to share in the pains of that conflict which in His case led to the Cross. This is our lot as it was His, and this means that faith is needful, and humility, and obedience, and the help of a heavenly arm, and the hope of a heavenly home. And the comfort of all this is assured to us if we suffer *with him*.

St. Paul explains the need to share in His sufferings as the condition of our sharing with Him in the inheritance of His glory. "We see Jesus . . . crowned with glory" after He had tasted death on the Cross (Heb. 2:9), and the Ascension from Olivet was a fitting sequel to the Atonement on Calvary. A company of disciples watched His ascent until He passed beyond the point of sight; then an angel escort saw Him return to the glory which had been His before the worlds were made. He sat down on the right hand of eternal majesty and He received the name which is above all other names, that at His name every knee should bow and every tongue should confess that He is Lord indeed. And that glory still waits for its final consummation at the end of this age when He will come again. Heaven and earth will then unite and will ascribe "blessing, and honour, and glory, and power" to Him for ever and ever (Rev. 5:13). But He will not enter upon this great glory alone, for the ultimate destiny of His brethren is that they will then be *glorified together* with Him; for "when Christ who is our life shall appear, then shall we also appear with him in glory" (Col. 3:4). The dead in Christ shall rise and those who are alive shall be transformed; all that is now mortal shall put on immortality, and we shall reign with Him in the glory of His kingdom. It is part of the great promise that we shall hear Him say: "Come, ye blessed of my Father; inherit the kingdom prepared for you from the foundation of the world" (Matt. 25:34). But such thoughts are almost too high for us, and we fall back on words of deep simplicity: "Beloved, now are we the sons of God, and it doth not yet appear what we shall be: but we know that when he shall appear, we shall be like him, for we shall see him as he is" (1 John 3:2).

St. Paul made use of a term *if so be* which was meant to stir up active self-inquiry (cf. 8:9).[1] All who rank as sons of God are fellow heirs with Christ and will share in His inheritance; but the fact of sonship means that they must suffer with Him as "the necessary antecedent" to share with Him in the inheritance of His glory. *And if children, then heirs; heirs of God, and joint-heirs with Christ; if so be that we suffer with him, that we may be also glorified with him* (R.V.). The great secret of fortitude and confidence for God's children in the crucible of such suffering is found in the double use of the phrase *with him*. It was only in the virtue of that union with Christ that St. Paul could write as he did and could look on from the present with such amazing buoyancy. He knew that to suffer with Christ would not lead to glory as a matter of merit or reward; but he also knew that it would help to enlarge all man's capacity to share in that glory. Few men have been called to submit to more pain in the school of trial for Christ's sake than St. Paul himself: not only in surrender and loss of earthly ambitions and possessions, not only in privation and affliction at the hands of others, not only in secret conflict with the devil's intrigues or in daily concern for the many churches, but in "always bearing about in the body the dying of the Lord Jesus" (2 Cor. 4:10). But none of these things could shake his faith in virtue of his union with Christ, for Christ in him was the hope of glory (Col. 1:27). It was almost as though he would call to mind a

[1] εἴπερ, cf. H. C. G. Moule: *Romans* (The Cambridge Bible), p. 148.

current saying which found voice in various expressions:[1] "If we be dead with him, we shall also live with him; if we suffer, we shall also reign with him" (2 Tim. 2:11,12). God counts all His sons as heirs; and all His heirs are princes; and all who are princes will be crowned when they share in "the inheritance of the saints in light" (Col. 1:12).

[1] W. Sanday and A. C. Headlam: op. cit., p. 204.

CHAPTER ELEVEN

Suffering and Glory

"For I reckon that the sufferings of this present time are not worthy to be compared with the glory which shall be revealed in us." (A.V.)

"For I reckon that the sufferings of this present time are not worthy to be compared with the glory which shall be revealed to us-ward." (R.V.)

"I consider that the sufferings of this present time are not worth comparing with the glory that is to be revealed to us." (R.S.V.)

—Romans 8:18

This verse follows out the connection between suffering and the hope of glory and shows that the trials of those who are sons of God are by no means inconsistent with their prospect in the future as heirs of God. St. Paul never lost sight of the ultimate destiny of those who are "in Christ Jesus" throughout this long chapter (cf. 8:1,39), and the whole trend of his thought had now set towards that theme "as the waters towards the moon".[1] God has never promised His sons and heirs freedom from suffering in the course of this world, and the experience of the Church is studded with the facts of trial and persecution. But the comfort of the children of God even in the darkest hours of pain and sorrow has been the hope of a glorious recompense in the future: *for I reckon that the sufferings*

[1] H. C. G. Moule: *Romans* (The Expositor's Bible), p. 226.

of this present time are not worthy to be compared with the glory which shall be revealed in us. St. Paul began with a favourite word which serves to demonstrate the full triumph of faith and hope: I *reckon.* That word spoke of ordinary calculation; it meant to weigh up in one's mind, to count what was in one column and to compare it with what was in the other. There was sublime insight in the choice of this word of cool, prosaic reckoning, for the problem of pain and the hope of glory touch chords in the heart which defy ordinary calculation. St. Paul used it with "the finest justness"[1] to state his strong personal conviction on a subject which goes beyond all the mathematics of mere profit or loss. "I think": that would have been too weak in view of the trials which he had already encountered. "I hope": that would have been too lame in view of the trials which were then painfully imminent. But I *reckon*: that would unite the past and the future and would be more moving in this context than the warmest language of poetry or emotion.[2]

The first column in this table of calculation is one of loss as a result of trial: *the sufferings of this present time.* It is of the very nature of sin that its evil results are felt by all alike, and there have been times when it seems as though the least guilty are those who most suffer. This has been a source of pain and conflict for God-fearing men all down the ages: they are perplexed and can find no answer until they go and stand in the sanctuary of God (cf. Ps. 73:16,17). There is only one bar where the wrongs of mankind will be redressed, and that is the bar of Him who will judge the world in righteousness and truth. But it was not to the sorrows of the world at large that St. Paul referred in this passage. His reference to sufferings was to the trials which must result from that union with Christ which makes men one with Him. They are members of His body, and they cannot escape from the pains of the head; when

[1] H. C. G. Moule: *Romans* (The Cambridge Bible), p. 148.
[2] H. C. G. Moule: *Romans* (The Expositor's Bible), p. 226.

one member suffers, all the other members suffer as well. But
the ultimate restriction of all such trial is made clear by the
phrase: *this present time*. St. Paul chose a word which would
show that he thought of time "not in its length, but in its limit"[1],
and the longest life of trial would therefore be no more than a
soon passing season compared with the life that will be crowned
with joy in eternity.

St. Paul's basic idea was that suffering in one form or another
belongs to the experience of all who are members of God's
household. Not all are martyrs; not all are captives; not all are
driven into exile for Christ's sake; not all are in fact called upon
to bear insult, scorn, or assault on the open stage of the world's
hostility. Many indeed are still so called, just as many were
called when St. Paul wrote these words, for the world is no
more in love with God and His children now than it was
before. And yet even those whose path has been most sheltered
in the goodness of God will be called to encounter suffering,
somehow, sometime, in the course of this life, if they are led
by the Spirit and live as sons of God. All His children will be
chastened with discipline and suffering in the loving wisdom
that rules their lives. It is a debt that they must pay, though its
form will vary as God may choose.[2] But to *suffer with him*
(8:17) will be enough to soften and sweeten the trial, for such
fellowship with Him now fits men for fellowship with Him
beyond *this present time* in glory. It was this thought that led
William Burns to exclaim with such ardent desire: "O that I
had a martyr's heart, if not a martyr's death and a martyr's
crown."[3]

The next column in this table of calculation is one of gain as
a result of hope: *the glory which shall be revealed in us*. St. Paul's
words look beyond the world of trial and point to the glory to

---

[1] καιρός, not χρόνος cf. H. C. G. Moule: op. cit., p. 226.
[2] Ibid., p. 225.
[3] Islay Burns: *Memoir of the Rev. William C. Burns*, p. 193.

come as a sober reality. This is not an idle fancy; it is the true consummation of all God's plans for the church and the world in the glorious universe which will comprise "a new heaven and a new earth" (Rev. 21:1). St. Paul's phrase, *which shall be revealed,* has a ring of uncommon emphasis in the Greek text;[1] it calls into use a special combination of verbs which would strengthen the main idea of destiny and certainty. It lays stress on the fact that this glory is destined, or certain, to be revealed, and the order of words in this phrase builds up the contrast with his earlier reference to *this present time.* He had spoken of *time* as a passing moment which is compressed within its own precise limits: it must begin; it must come to an end. But there are no limits to the promised *glory*: it cannot be measured; it will endure when time itself shall be no more. This was the great prospect which caught and held his heart and mind in the midst of pain and sorrow: such things would fade from sight in view of the glory that will yet be revealed.

St. Paul's mighty concept was that glory will be commensurate with the timeless future that is yet to unfold and will transcend all that the sons of God can now conceive. "Eye hath not seen, nor ear heard, neither have entered into the heart of man, the things which God hath prepared for them that love him" (1 Cor. 2:9). There is another utterance which serves as a commentary on the whole of this great dictum: "Our light affliction, which is but for a moment, worketh for us a far more exceeding and eternal weight of glory" (2 Cor. 4:17). That verse is a studied contrast of such colossal magnitude that it almost beggars the use of words. St. Paul measured the light burdens of trial with the massive weight of glory and saw that trial is the merest trifle in view of the glory it will procure. Such trial is but for a moment and will come to an end, whereas glory has an eternal character and will increase exceedingly. And this glory which will so far surpass all our

[1] τὴν μέλλουσαν δόξαν ἀποκαλυφθῆναι.

present tribulation will be revealed *in us*; it will shine *to us-ward* (R.V.) in the presence of God. It was this hope that made Samuel Rutherford exclaim in a mingled outburst of reverie and rhapsody: "Glory, glory dwelleth in Immanuel's land!"[1]

St. Paul's line of advance from his initial reckoning to his ultimate conclusion is marked by a vigorous emphasis in his bold phrase: *not worthy to be compared*. He had added up the tables of loss in the present and gain in the future, and it needed no long-drawn-out calculation to tell that the sorrows of time hardly deserve a thought in view of the glory in store. They are not worth considering in a comparison in which the two sides are so far out of mutual proportion: for how can the little affairs of time hope to balance the mighty facts of eternity? St. Paul's words not only make it clear that temporal affliction is no equivalent to the promised glory; they show that it will sink into total oblivion when the children of God enter into their great inheritance. Such calculation and comparison were based on the facts of his own experience, and he was as sure of it all as if it could be proved by the ordinary rules of mathematics. He was as much alive to the problems of pain as any man may be, but it was the logic of faith rather than of feeling which led him to form this judgment: *for I reckon that the sufferings of this present time are not worthy to be compared with the glory which shall be revealed in us*. This was a ray of light for those who were enmeshed in the darkness of an age of persecution. They were "partakers of his sufferings" (1 Pet. 4:13) but they rejoiced that they were to become "partakers of the glory that shall be revealed" (1 Pet. 5:1). Such a hope has infused strength and comfort into the hearts of men like John Calvin in the face of grievous adversity. It was indeed with this verse on his lips, but in such pain that he could not finish the words, that he died with sure and certain hope of glory in the arms of Beza.[2]

[1] Andrew Bonar: *Letters of Samuel Rutherford, with a Sketch of His Life*, p. 22.
[2] H. C. G. Moule: *Romans* (The Cambridge Bible), p. 149.

CHAPTER TWELVE

The Whole Created Universe

"For the earnest expectation of the creature waiteth for the manifestation of the sons of God. For the creature was made subject to vanity, not willingly, but by reason of him who hath subjected the same in hope, because the creature itself also shall be delivered from the bondage of corruption into the glorious liberty of the children of God." (A.V.)

"For the earnest expectation of the creation waiteth for the revealing of the sons of God. For the creation was subjected to vanity, not of its own will, but by reason of him who subjected it, in hope that the creation itself also shall be delivered from the bondage of corruption into the liberty of the glory of the children of God." (R.V.)

"For the creation waits with eager longing for the revealing of the sons of God; for the creation was subjected to futility, not of its own will but by the will of him who subjected it in hope; because the creation itself will be set free from its bondage to decay and obtain the glorious liberty of the children of God." (R.S.V.)

— Romans 8:19–21

This great passage elaborates St. Paul's teaching on the problem of pain and the hope of glory in a magnificent view of the whole natural creation. This is made clear by the cosmic significance of the word which he wove into each verse.[1] It is true that there are times when this word may have a more limited reference; it may denote mankind rather than the inanimate world of nature (cf. Mark 16:15; Col. 1:23). If this were its meaning in this passage, it would point to the vague longings in the heart of humanity for a better and more wholesome future. But this meaning is quite inadequate as an explanation of the sweep of Pauline thought and vision in this context. He saw the whole natural creation as in contrast with the children of God, and spoke of it as though it were full of eager expectation for a coming glory which it will share with them.[2] St. Paul employed language of great intensity, and it reflects something of man's feelings as a conscious being. There were poetic qualities in his penetrating insight which taught him to see the marks of imperfection in the world of nature as a visible expression of a lack which will at length be made good.[3] Thus he ascribed to it the force of a hidden language and he discerned in it the voice of a buried anguish. Such language was figurative, but was similar to the pictorial imagery which Old Testament writers had so freely employed. He saw the griefs and wrongs in the present order of things as a figure of the longings in the world of nature and he made it clear that the whole created universe will share in the glory of those who are heirs of God and joint-heirs with Christ. This grand cosmic vision adds a vivid colour to the glorious destiny which is reserved for those who will "appear with him" (Col. 3:4).

The first word *for* ushers in a profound reason for the

[1] $\varkappa\tau\iota\sigma\iota\varsigma$ ("creature" in A.V.; "creation" in R.V. and R.S.V.).
[2] H. C. G. Moule: op cit., pp. 149–50.
[3] W. Sanday and A. C. Headlam: op. cit., p. 207.

F

measured calculation of the last verse: *for the earnest expectation of the creation waiteth for the manifestation of the sons of God.* This bold picture of the world of nature in a state of *earnest expectation* has an imaginative quality which is hard to resist. St. Paul used a forceful compound word which gave a heightened appeal to the feelings described.[1] Its root meaning suggests a man standing up on tip-toe, straining forward to catch a glimpse of a person for whose coming he has longed with ardent desire (cf. Phil. 1:20). Such a word clothes the whole natural creation with an almost human feeling as it now waits out the present time in hope of future glory. This is followed by a similar example of a compound structure in the verb which depicts nature as "absorbed in waiting".[2] What does it wait for with such eager longing? *The manifestation of the sons of God.* St. Paul caught up a word from the last verse and used it as a noun to sum up the prospect in store for those who have suffered with Him.[3] Glory will be revealed as theirs, and they will be revealed to each other: and their authentic character as the sons of God will be made clear to the whole created universe. Nor was that all; the eye of faith saw their advent to this glory as the mysterious crisis which will also bring a healing benediction to the present order of things. This was why St. Paul could ascribe to the world as a whole that deep sense of expectation which the Psalmist sought to evoke when the king was at hand: "Let the heavens rejoice and let the earth be glad; . . . for he cometh, for he cometh to judge the earth: he shall judge the world with righteousness and the people with his truth" (Ps. 96:11,13).

The same word *for* begins the next verse and explains why the world of nature should be on the tip-toe of such earnest longing: *for the creation was made subject to vanity, not willingly, but*

---

[1] ἀποκαραδοκία.

[2] ἀπεκδέκεται cf. H. C. G. Moule: op. cit., p. 150.

[3] ἀποκαλυφθῆναι (8:18); ἀποκάλυψις (8:19).

by reason of him who hath subjected the same in hope. The plain historical significance of this statement is stressed by the aorist tense of the verb[1] which points back to man's Fall as the cause of the curse which came upon the earth. The whole natural creation had been pronounced good and stable until man's sin brought in all the marks of wreck and ruin. The long-drawn-out echo of the word of judgment may still be heard: "Cursed is the ground for thy sake" (Gen. 3:17). A change for the worse came over the world when it was made subject to *vanity,* to weariness and frustration. All that was once good now bears the marks of evil; and this evil in the material world of nature is a mysterious sequel to the evil in the moral world of humanity. There is a more intimate connection than we can now define between man's sin and the decay to which the whole universe is now liable.[2] But this was an unwilling subjection; it was not a voluntary situation, induced by its own choice or of its own accord. There had been no inherent demerit in the world that God made; the curse that came upon it had been for man's sake. This means that the present state of things is not in accord with the original course of nature; it springs from the decree *of him who hath subjected the same in hope.* This must refer to God as the Judge who pronounced the curse, and it means that in God's purpose that vanity or frustration was not final.[3] The world which was involved in man's ruin shares with man the promise of a glorious redemption; the curse was not beyond recall, for there is yet the hope of a magnificent recovery.

The next verse was meant to confirm this hope as a goal that will be achieved in the fulness of time: *because the creation itself also shall be delivered from the bondage of corruption into the glorious liberty of the children of God.* The word *because* (A.V.; R.S.V.)

[1] ὑπετ η.
[2] H. C. G. Moule: *Romans* (The Expositor's Bible), p. 228.
[3] Charles Hodge: op. cit., p. 272.

may equally be translated as *that* (R.V.),[1] and the object in each case is to point to God's plan to liberate creation from bondage and decay. The phrase *itself also* stresses the fact that the created universe as well as the children of God will share in that beneficent design to lift the curse. This will result in its deliverance from bondage and decay and its restoration to freedom and glory. The day of bondage in which physical corruption rules all nature will end with the revocation of the curse which was laid on the earth for man's sake; the day of freedom in which divine splendour will clothe the world will dawn with the revelation of the glory which is reserved for the children of God. This will mean the dissolution of the now fallen world in something like an atomic explosion (2 Pet. 3:10), and the re-creation of the heavens and the earth in paramount majesty (Rev. 21:1). St. Paul did not expand this train of thought; it was incidental to his main theme. His great primary intention was to furnish the most vivid idea of the glorious destiny that lies before the sons of God; this was enhanced by the thought that the whole created universe will be set free from its present waste and futility when that goal is attained. The phrase *glorious liberty* is an imperfect translation because it inverts the order of thought: the words point to glory as the predominant idea and to freedom as a subordinate factor.[2] The whole world will enter upon the freedom of glory with the children of God.

This great doctrine of a cosmic fall and recovery is clear from the singular connection between the first three chapters of Genesis and the last three chapters of the Revelation. The long journey from one to the other follows a track which is like the perimeter of a golden circle. It starts with the narrative of the first creation, and the rivers that watered the garden, and the

---

[1] διότι or ὅτι.

[2] τὴν ἐλευθερίαν τῆς δόξης, cf. W. Sanday and A. C. Headlam: op. cit., p. 208.

tree of life, and the daily tryst between man and his Maker; and then it tells of the serpent whose trail lies everywhere, and the sin of disobedience, and the curse that came by sin; and it goes on to show how man was driven out of Eden, and that earthly Paradise was lost, and a sword of fire was set up to turn in every direction so as to guard the way to the tree of life. That sword of fire was meant to throw a ring of flame round the garden; it was like a blazing girdle. What could be so full of menace as sword and fire in one? It would threaten instant death for any man who tried to return to the garden by his own self-effort; and yet it would preserve it all as if to show that God purposed to bring man home at length to the glorious paradise on high. It was in the desert of man's sin that the Son of Man came to sheathe that sword in His own body and to open the gates to the Kingdom of God.

> " 'Twas here the Lord of Life appeared,
>   And sighed, and groaned, and prayed, and feared;
>   Bore all incarnate God could bear,
>   With strength enough, and none to spare."

But He has made possible a new creation, the new heavens and the new earth. Here flows the pure river of the water of life, clear as crystal; here stands the tree whose leaves shall be for the healing of the nations; here shall God's servants see His face. And there is one other feature: "There shall be no more curse" (Rev. 22:3).

CHAPTER THIRTEEN

The Pains of Birth

"For we know that the whole creation groaneth and travaileth in pain together until now. And not only they, but ourselves also, which have the firstfruits of the Spirit, even we ourselves groan within ourselves, waiting for the adoption, to wit, the redemption of our body." (A.V.)

"For we know that the whole creation groaneth and travaileth in pain together until now. And not only so, but ourselves also, which have the firstfruits of the Spirit, even we ourselves groan within ourselves, waiting for our adoption, to wit, the redemption of our body." (R.V.)

"We know that the whole creation has been groaning in travail together until now; and not only the creation, but we ourselves, who have the firstfruits of the Spirit, groan inwardly as we wait for adoption as sons, the redemption of our bodies." (R.S.V.)

—Romans 8:22–3

St. Paul had turned aside from his main theme about present trial and coming glory for the children of God and had drawn an illustration of the greatness of that glory from the prospect which lies before the whole created universe. Then his thought swung back to focus itself on the pain and travail which are common to the world of nature and to the sons of God before they can attain to the glorious destiny which He has planned for them. There is a strong poetic element in the candour as well as the insight of this comparison: it is marked by striking realism in the groans of childbirth which break out in the midst of a song of glory.[1] He had observed "the pathos and sorrow" which abound in nature; he saw them as the signs of a travail like that which comes upon a woman in labour.[2] It is as though the world sighs for release from the convulsive agony of the ages; but this is a sigh of hope as well as of pain. This is made clear by St. Paul's choice of a word that spoke of the pangs of birth, not of the throes of death, and it is the hope of new life which gives meaning to that travail and turns sorrow into great joy. This is no less true of all God's children who groan within themselves but who cherish the hope of a full and final deliverance when the day of glory appears. St. Paul used the same bold obstetric metaphor in one other passage as an illustration of the spiritual birth-pangs which he had to endure for those who were like his children and for whom he travailed in birth again so that Christ might be formed in them (Gal. 4:19). The whole created universe and the children of God are now in the hour of labour; but they will think no more of its anguish in the day of glory at hand (John 16:21).

St. Paul began with the word *for* in a statement which explains and confirms what goes before: *for we know that the whole creation groaneth and travaileth in pain together until now*. He spoke of facts which were common knowledge, though a proper understanding of them may have been less common than he supposed.[3] *We know:* we see from the facts of "universal and long continued experience";[4] we know from our observation of the pain and tension which are everywhere manifest in the world of nature. We cannot close our eyes to the fact

[1] H. C. G. Moule: op. cit., p. 228.   [2] A. M. Hunter: op. cit., p. 82.
[3] W. Sanday and A. C. Headlam: op. cit., pp. 208-9.
[4] Charles Hodge: op. cit., p. 273.

that the whole created universe is a sounding board which emits a groan, and that groan speaks of a heavy burden and a weary longing. A world that groans would have offered a bold enough picture; it is even bolder when it is linked with the idea that this is a cry of travail. The groaning is interpreted by the further picture of a world in labour like a woman whose hour has come. St. Paul chose a powerful metaphor in order to explain why the whole world should groan in pain; it was the same image which the Lord had used when He spoke of "the beginnings of sorrows" (Mark 13:8). This is made clear in the modern version: "the birth-pangs of the new age begin" (N.E.B.). The word *together* must be taken with the two verbs, *groaneth and travaileth in pain*,[1] and it refers to the whole vast complex of the natural creation; "it groans *in all its parts* as if in the pangs of childbirth" (N.E.B.). But where there is present distress, there is also hope for future comfort; the phrase *until now* hints at the great change from one to the other.[2] That phrase covers the whole of time from the original subjugation of the world of nature to the present moment. It has groaned from the day when the curse came upon the earth; but the groaning will cease when the new age is born.

St. Paul's next words are an emphatic assertion of the fact that our own experience is not dissimilar: *and not only they, but ourselves also, which have the firstfruits of the Spirit, even we ourselves groan within ourselves.* The phrase *not only they* should be rendered *not only so* as in the Revised Version:[3] it is the bridge from the unconscious creation to the living members of God's household. There is tremendous insistence in the repetition of the pronoun: *but ourselves also ... even we ourselves*; it is as though he would invest the truth with as strong a personal element as words permit. Its meaning is defined by the qualifying parenthesis: *which have the firstfruits of the Spirit*. This is the first mention of the Spirit in this passage on the fact of sorrow

[1] συνστενάζει καὶ συνωδίνει.   [2] ἄχρι τοῦ νῦν.   [3] οὐ μόνον δέ.

and the hope of glory, but the comfort of His presence was never far absent from the realities of trial which St. Paul had in view. We are the sons of God, and we have the Spirit; sonship and the Spirit are inseparable in this context (cf. 8:9,14). St. Paul borrowed the image of firstfruits from the ancient custom of a thank-offering at the time of harvest (cf. 11:16; 16:5). Its most famous use was in his chapter on the resurrection of those who sleep in death: "Christ the firstfruits; afterward they that are Christ's at his coming" (1 Cor. 15:23). St. Paul had made it clear before that we have the Spirit in a way that others do not (cf. 8:9); now he made it clear that we have the Spirit as the pledge and promise of the harvest which is yet to follow. But we who are the sons of God and who have the Spirit, *even we ourselves groan within ourselves*. St. John used a similar expression about the Son of Man who "groaned in the spirit" at the sight of human distress (John 11:33,38),[1] and St. Paul's choice of this forceful word would express his sense of the heavy burden which lies on our inmost spirit.[2] We groan within, because the burden itself is inward.

St. Paul's last clause shows that such groans are not those of despair, but of earnest expectation: *waiting for the adoption, to wit, the redemption of our body*. The word *waiting* is the same as the word which he had used of the natural creation (8:19): we wait for the same great consummation for which it waits, and that is the full and final declaration of our sonship. This is the last reference in this chapter to our *adoption*, and it refers to the recognition of our status as sons in the day of glory. St. Paul alternated between *sons* and *children* throughout the whole of this passage (8:14-23):[3] his use of such terms was almost synonymous, but the underlying idea of *adoption* was dominant.

---

[1] ἐνεβριμήσατο.
[2] στενάζομεν.
[3] υἱοί (8:14, 19); τέκνα (8:16, 17, 21).
[4] υἱοθεσία (8:15, 23).

This verse sums up the great hope that marks our sonship and draws added meaning from a comparable passage in the Galatian epistle (Gal. 4:1–7). Now we are like minors; then, in the full sense, we shall be adults: we shall enter upon the full inheritance of our status as sons, to which meanwhile we look forward with an intense desire. St. Paul went on to add words of definition which would explain what this glorious destiny implies: *to wit, the redemption of our body.* This quick passage of thought from *adoption* to *redemption* does not mean that the two words are identical in their meaning, but that the first is an experience which is necessary for the second. The Son of God who took on Him a true human body and bore it up into heaven is not ashamed to own us as brethren, and our ultimate redemption will only be complete when our mortal bodies have been fashioned anew like "the body of his glory" (Phil. 3:21 R.V.).[1] Those who have the firstfruits of the Spirit have in themselves the pledge that He who raised up Christ from the dead shall also quicken their now mortal bodies in the hour of resurrection (8:11) and their manifestation as the sons of God will be complete.

This ends the great analogy, but its parallels are so instructive that they deserve thorough recognition. The whole created universe groans, and we groan; but where there is travail, there is also expectation. Nature waits, and we wait; and what each waits for is the full declaration of our sonship. This will mean the "restitution of all things" in the world around (Acts 3:21) and the resurrection of the dead from the grave itself. The whole world joins in a common sigh and shares a common travail because it has always been kept straining forward to the age of glory; perhaps it is not too much to say that the earth groans in travail, sighing for the hour of deliverance from the dust of the saints carried in its womb all down the ages. And all that we ourselves feel and bear in hidden travail is wrapped up with

[1] H. C. G. Moule: *Romans* (The Cambridge Bible), p. 152.

the tensions and yearnings of our mortality; we long for the hour of release when our bodies are set free from the last traces of sin and death (cf. 8:2). Then our adoption will be manifest to all, and our redemption will be perfected; the great day of freedom and of glory will have dawned for ever. St. Paul's recognition of "the birth-pangs of the new age" (Mark 13:8 N.E.B.) and their comparison with our experience is in itself remarkable, but it also reveals his own wise and sober judgment in a strictly spiritual domain.[1] He could rejoice in the fact that he was an heir of God and a joint-heir with Christ, but he would not pretend to an unreal situation. He still had a mortal body, weak, frail, subject to pain and death: "in this, we groan" (2 Cor. 5:2). And this body was the outward vestment of a fallen nature: in this also, he groaned (Rom. 7:24). But such groaning was not in vain: it was part of the pangs which must be felt before new life is born, and the prospect of such new life filled the hour of travail with meaning and purpose.

[1] H. C. G. Moule: *Romans* (The Expositor's Bible), pp. 228–9.

CHAPTER FOURTEEN

The Hope of Glory

"For we are saved by hope: but hope that is seen is not hope: for what a man seeth, why doth he yet hope for? But if we hope for that we see not, then do we with patience wait for it."   (A.V.)

"For by hope were we saved: but hope that is seen is not hope: for who hopeth for that which he seeth? But if we hope for that which we see not, then do we with patience wait for it."   (R.V.)

"For in this hope we were saved. Now hope that is seen is not hope. For who hopes for what he sees? But if we hope for what we do not see, we wait for it with patience."   (R.S.V.)

—Romans 8:24–5

St. Paul's eyes were fastened on the coming glories which will mark our ultimate salvation, and he caught up the word *hope* which he had used in passing (cf. 8:20) to show how we can bear all our present trials with patience. This word occurs three times as a noun and twice as a verb in these two short verses and drums itself into our minds in the English versions by their monosyllabic translation of the Greek text. St. Paul's object was to insist that the distinctive attitude of the children of God in the midst of all trial is that of hope, and hope which is rooted in God Himself implies that there is far more to come than all that is in actual possession. He used the word *hope* for *the thing hoped for,* just as he had used the word *creation* for *the thing created* (cf. 8:19 etc.), and this passage defines what this thing is by its repeated reference to the prospect which is in store: "The glory which shall be revealed in us" (8:18); "the manifestation of the sons of God" (8:19); "the glorious liberty of the children of God" (8:21); "the adoption, to wit, the redemption of our body" (8:23). It is this last phrase which forms the immediate antecedent of this passage, for our ultimate redemption draws our vision forward to the complete deliverance of body and spirit from sin and death (cf. 8:2). This will not be achieved until both body and spirit have been reunited in each wholly redeemed being on the day of resurrection. This is *the hope* which is "laid up" (Col. 1:5) or "set before" (Heb. 6:18) the sons of God, and the definite article in the Greek text[1] suggests that it must be seen as coincident with "that blessed hope" which will be fulfilled in "the glorious appearing of the great God and our Saviour Jesus Christ" (Titus 2:13).[2] Therefore the fact that Christ is "in you" now is "the hope of glory" (Col. 1:27).

The first word *for* provides the link in St. Paul's line of thought: *for we are saved by hope.* Salvation is a term which may have reference to the past, the present, or the future: we have been saved from the guilt which sin entails; we are being saved from the power which sin exerts; we shall be saved from the taint which sin involves. This term in its total meaning includes all three facets, and it always implies the two distinct ideas of danger and rescue. In the case of this verse, the verb must be explained in the light of its link with the idea of hope, and a literal translation of the whole clause is of direct value: *for we were saved in hope.* We were in grave danger of sin and death; we have now been rescued by an act of mercy and grace. But our experience of that saving mercy is as yet no more than partial; the full blessing of that glorious salvation belongs to the future.

---

[1] ἡ ἐλπίς.   [2] Cf. H. C. G. Moule: op. cit., p. 229.

This is why it is a matter of hope for which we must wait with patient expectation. The case of the word *hope* is not meant to express the means by which the thing is done, but the circumstances in which it will occur.[1] St. Paul's custom was to link man's experience of God's saving mercy with an act of grace on God's side and an act of faith on man's side (cf. 3:24,28; Eph. 2:8,9). This connection is emphatic and it makes it certain that the correct reading in this phrase is that we were saved *in hope*. We do not now have in actual possession the full benefits of our salvation, but we live in the hope that we are yet to share in the ultimate fruition of the saving process. The work of grace and the life of faith will yet be crowned with final glory, and it is in respect of that great hope that we were saved.

St. Paul's next words argue that hope refers to the unseen and the future: *but hope that is seen is not hope; for what a man seeth, why doth he yet hope for?* Hope is the daughter of experience (cf. 5:4) and the sister of faith and love (1 Cor. 13:13), and it belongs to the nature of hope that it directs its gaze towards things future and unseen.[2] Hope cannot be identified with sight, because something which has come to the point of sight is no longer a thing to be hoped for. Once the thing is seen as present, the work of hope is at an end: if it be the one, it cannot be the other. This is enforced by the next clause: *for who hopes for what he sees* (R.S.V.)? Both the Revised and the Revised Standard Versions adopt this short reading, and it makes an immediate impact which the longer reading fails to convey. The thing for which we hope is the full and glorious salvation which the Gospel reveals; that must be an object of hope because it is bound up with a promise. That promise is grounded in the absolute faithfulness of God Himself, but it has not yet been fulfilled. It is certain, though yet unseen; it is valid, though yet future. This means that hope is an essential element in the "earnest expectation" which makes men strain

[1] Charles Hodge: op. cit., p. 275.   [2] Loc. cit.

forward to "the glorious liberty of the children of God"
(8:19,21). "We look, not at the things which are seen, but at
the things which are not seen: for the things which are seen are
temporal; but the things which are not seen are eternal" (2 Cor.
4:18). Such hope is an active, buoyant, cheerful reality in the
experience of the hard-pressed pilgrim: he will hold on his way
in spite of all adversity as one who has learnt to "rejoice in hope
of the glory of God" (5:2).

The last words turn to the practical connection of hope with
the present situation: *but if we hope for that we see not, then do we
with patience wait for it.* We are now men of hope; the goal towards which we look is still out of sight: but our hope is
as sure as that of men who look for the sunrise;[1] therefore
it becomes the mainspring of intent and patient waiting.
Patience looks back to the persecution of "the present time"
and forward to "the glory which shall be revealed" (8:18): it
is the great virtue of steadfastness and fortitude which helps
men to endure trial and darkness, knowing that "joy cometh in
the morning" (Ps. 30:5). Hope and patience are linked elsewhere in a reciprocal spirit (cf. 5:4; 12:12; 15:4; 1 Thess. 1:3),
and this inter-action is the secret which makes men stand on
the tip-toe of strong expectation. St. Paul caught up the word
wait which he had twice used in this passage (8:19,23), and
let it speak with quiet finality. There is nothing supine in this
spirit; it is not the kind of nerveless mood that resigns itself to
the burdens of the moment. It speaks of a strong and active
desire which looks forward with an eager delight to the promised event. Therefore hope and patience unite to make men
wait for the glory which is as yet unseen but which is as sure
as the dawn. And that glory is not a vague, abstract ideal; it
is centred in the return of Christ Himself. It is when Christ
who is our life shall appear that we also shall appear with
Him in glory (Col. 3:4). It is in this hope that we were saved;

[1] H. C. G. Moule: op. cit., p. 230

it is for this hope that we now wait. It is hard to emasculate the word in the smallest degree; it points to nothing less than His return.[1]

The last promise in the Bible evoked from St. John the Divine words of ardent welcome: "Amen! Even so, come, Lord Jesus" (Rev. 22:20). This descent from heaven will be a true reversal of the Ascension; it will be the return of a living person in like manner as when He went away (Acts 1:11). The hope of His return has brought solace to the persecuted and strength to His people in all ages. Their faith may be summed up in the words of the Psalm: "My soul waiteth for the Lord more than they that watch for the morning" (Ps. 130:6). This was finely illustrated in the life of Dr. Horatius Bonar, the great Scottish preacher, poet, and hymn-writer, whose whole ministry had been warmed and inspired by the promise of His coming. During a long illness before he died at the age of eighty in July 1889, his eyes constantly rested on the text which hung on the wall at the foot of his bed: "Until the day break, and the shadows flee away" (Song of Sol. 2:17; 4:6). Those words brought him endless comfort, and were inscribed on his tomb in the heart of the city where he was born and where he died.[2] And so too it was in 1924 when Mr. Horace E. B. Young of Fairymead, Bundaberg, a man of God greatly honoured in the business world and greatly beloved in his own home circle, lay dying in North Queensland. His wife sat by the bed throughout the night, and while it was yet dark, his life moved to its close. She left the room and went outside to stand on the hospital verandah, and as she looked away towards the hills, she saw the gleam of dawn light up in the sky. The night had gone; a new day had begun to breathe; and she thankfully realised that separation was only "until the day break and the shadows flee away". Jesus Himself is "the

[1] H.C.G. Moule: op. cit., p. 229, fn. 2.
[2] See Horatius Bonar: *Until The Day Break* (Introduction, pp. ix–x).

dayspring from on high" (Luke 1:78), "the bright and morning star" (Rev. 22:16): therefore hope still stands on tip-toe, waiting "until the day dawn, and the day-star arise" (2 Peter 1:19).

CHAPTER FIFTEEN

The Spirit and Our Weakness

"Likewise the Spirit also helpeth our infirmities: for we know not what we should pray for as we ought: but the Spirit itself maketh intercession for us with groanings which cannot be uttered. And he that searcheth the hearts knoweth what is the mind of the Spirit, because he maketh intercession for the saints according to the will of God." (A.V.)

"And in like manner the Spirit also helpeth our infirmity: for we know not how to pray as we ought; but the Spirit himself maketh intercession for us with groanings which cannot be uttered; and he that searcheth the hearts knoweth what is the mind of the Spirit, because he maketh intercession for the saints according to the will of God." (R.V.)

"Likewise the Spirit helps us in our weakness; for we do not know how to pray as we ought, but the Spirit himself intercedes for us with sighs too deep for words. And he who searches the hearts of men knows what is the mind of the Spirit, because the Spirit intercedes for the saints according to the will of God." (R.S.V.)

—Romans 8:26–7

This long section on the Spirit and our sonship, on present adversity and coming glory, moves to a close with this final statement about the work of the Holy Spirit. It provides an echo of more than one idea which had been in debate, and the heartfelt groan which drags through nature and haunts the sons of God is still painfully audible. St. Paul knew it only too well; it was in fact his own. He had pointed to the hope of glory as a wonderful antidote for our present distress; now he would point to the living presence of the Holy Spirit as the mighty source of strength and comfort in our current weakness:[1] *likewise the Spirit also helpeth our infirmities: for we know not what we should pray for as we ought: but the Spirit himself (R.V.) maketh intercession for us with groanings which cannot be uttered.* St. Paul knew that there are times when men sink into silence through the very intensity of their desires, and times when they are so conscious of the burdens of their mortality that they can do nothing but groan with sighs too deep for words.[2] But he would have us know that we are not "alone in our struggles",[3] for the Spirit Himself takes hold of us in our perplexity: we may be at a loss for words, but He can lend intelligence to our desires. It is as though He were Himself to speak through our wordless longing, and His voice must be heard: *and he that searcheth the hearts knoweth what is the mind of the Spirit, because he maketh intercession for the saints according to the will of God.* It is a fact that it belongs to God alone to search the heart; therefore He is able to interpret and understand its least articulate desire: when that desire reflects the mind of the Spirit, it is bound to prevail: it is spiritual intercession which must reflect the will of God.

St. Paul still had in mind the help that comes from a clear view of the ground and object of hope, and that prompted him

---

[1] H. C. G. Moule: op. cit., p. 232.
[2] J. R. W. Stott: op. cit., p. 124.
[3] W. Sanday and A. C. Headlam: op. cit., 212.

to speak of another reservoir of strength and calm: *likewise the Spirit also helpeth our infirmities: for we know not what we should pray for as we ought.* The word *likewise, in the same way,* shows how St. Paul strove to pile one reason for confidence on another: as hope sustains the sons of God, so the Spirit helps them in their weakness. He does not remove the cause of groaning, but He does support them in their travail. He is ready to help like an unseen friend who stands by their side and takes their hand into his own firm clasp. It is identical with the word which Martha had used: "Bid her therefore that she *help* me" (Luke 10:40).[1] This is very appropriate in a context where the Holy Spirit is represented as condescending to take upon Himself some part of our burden so as to relieve us of its pressure.[2] The word *infirmity* (R.V.) combines the two ideas of weakness and burden (cf. Heb. 4:15): we have heavy burdens to bear, and but little strength to bear them (cf. Matt. 11:28). Thus it includes all that disrupts patient waiting, such as weakness, absence of strength, and in particular, helpless indecision in prayer.[3] St. Paul did not suggest that we have no knowledge of what it means to pray, but that we do not know *how to pray as we ought* (R.V.; R.S.V.); the real problem is not what to pray for, but how to pray at all. The deep inward longing of a man's heart may be hard to define in words, and he may be keenly aware of the lack of coherent utterance. If the world of nature groans in travail, can the children of God escape from its manifold suffering? No, they cannot; but the Spirit Himself will draw near to impart strength to their soul even when they falter so much that they do not know how to pray.

It is in such an hour of felt weakness that the Holy Spirit draws near to act for us in grace: *but the Spirit himself maketh intercession for us with groanings which cannot be uttered* (R.V.). There are crises in life when all human strength turns into

---

[1] συναντιλαμβάνω.   [2] Charles Hodge: op. cit., 276.
[3] H. C. G. Moule: *Romans* (The Cambridge Bible), p. 153.

weakness; it is then that, left to ourselves, we find that we do not even know how to pray. But the Holy Spirit is the divine source and spring of intercession in our inmost being and He moves in the soul in such a way that His mysterious groaning mingles with ours.[1] We find that we are not alone even when we groan with wordless longing: the groan of the Spirit pervades as the groan of nature reflects all the secret anguish in such a *cri de cœur*. St. Paul's language is that of a bold and anthropomorphic imagination when he ascribes to the Spirit such real human activities as these groans of intercession. But it does not weaken the force of his idea if we admit that its fundamental meaning is that He breathes in and through our scarcely articulate desires. It is not that He prays and groans in the manner of men, but that He is said to do just what we are caused by Him to do.[2] Not all prayer is formulated in words or is articulate in thought: there are sighs that lie too deep for words just as there is sorrow that runs too deep for tears. True prayer may or may not find voice in words: even when it is most articulate, it may have its root in desires that cannot be uttered. But the Holy Spirit will impart a meaning to such desires which they would not have of themselves; He will clothe them with a "shape and value" which is altogether beyond all that we can define.[3] He draws out our longings towards the will of God by this inward activity which is as distinct as it is unique: it is comparable with His activity when He constrains the heart to cry, as it would not cry if left to itself, Abba, Father (8:15).

There is a strong underlying reason why such intercession is not in vain even though it may have little meaning in the ears of the world: *and he that searcheth the hearts knoweth what is the mind of the Spirit, because he maketh intercession for the saints*

[1] H. C. G. Moule: *Romans* (The Expositor's Bible), p. 232.
[2] Charles Hodge: op. cit., p. 277.
[3] W. Sanday and A. C. Headlam: op. cit., p. 214.

according to the will of God. The fact that it belongs to God alone
to search the heart is made clear in Scripture: He alone can
forgive and He alone can judge. This prerogative is delegated
by the Father to none except His Son: "All the churches shall
know that I am he which searcheth the reins and hearts"
(Rev. 2:23). He looks below the surface and sees to the very
bottom of things; He discerns the motives which prompt the
most faltering utterance and knows *the mind of the Spirit* (cf.
8:6, R.V.). This is followed by a final clause which explains
that He knows and welcomes the mind of the Spirit because
the mind of the Spirit in the work of intercession is in line with
the will of God. He can interpret the mind of the Spirit, and
the Spirit can reinforce our prayers. It is interesting to compare
the office of the Spirit who makes intercession within with the
office of Christ who makes intercession above: it is the work of
the Spirit to guide and mould our thoughts in prayer, while
it is the work of our great High Priest to act as our Mediator
in the presence of God (cf. 8:34). He makes intercession
within when our prayers are in the Spirit (Eph. 6:18). The
word *saints* takes the place of the earlier reference to the *sons or
children* of God, and it points to the distinctive character of those
who have the mind of the Spirit. His mind always reflects the
will of God and is free from all the errors which may pervade
our prayers: therefore to pray in the Spirit is to prevail with
God. "This is the confidence that we have in him, that if we
ask anything according to his will, he heareth us: and if we
know that he hear us, whatsoever we ask, we know that we
have the petitions that we desired of him" (1 John 5:14–15).

We ought not to lose sight of the tremendous parallels in
this passage, for they serve to show how the grace of God can
meet the need of men. As we groan, so He groans, and this
gives a meaning to our trembling desires which they did not
possess before. As hope sustains, so He sustains, and this provides a source of strength which is more than a match for our

weakness. This is seen in His work as the one who inspires the spirit of supplication after the will of God. St. Paul could write from the wealth of his own experience: it was fourteen years since he had besought the Lord that the thorn in the flesh might be removed. God did not grant that prayer in the manner that he desired, but gave him a yet more mighty answer in the promise that His grace would more than suffice for all his need (2 Cor. 12:9). So it was with Monica when she besought the Lord with cries and tears to stay Augustine from his plan to leave home. God did not grant that prayer in the manner that she desired, but the son of those tears could not perish and He gave her all her desire when Augustine was converted through the preaching of Ambrose in Milan.[1] So it was with David Brainerd when he besought the Lord in an agony of prayer for the Indians by their camp-fires or their wigwams. "I was in such an agony from sun half an hour high till near dark", so he wrote on June 14th, 1742, "that I was all over wet with sweat; but . . . my dear Jesus did sweat blood for poor souls. I longed for more compassion."[2] The thrice repeated cry of St. Paul, the tears of Monica, and the anguish in the heart of David Brainerd were not unlike the "strong crying and tears" which shook the frame of Him who "being in an agony . . . prayed more earnestly" (cf. Heb. 5:7; Luke 22:44). God can never ignore those *sighs too deep for words* which are constrained by His Spirit in the midst of weakness, perplexity, and need.

[1] H. C. G. Moule: op. cit., p. 233.
[2] Jonathan Edwards: *Complete Works,* vol. iii, pp. 110–11.

CHAPTER SIXTEEN

All Things . . . For Good

"And we know that all things work together for good to them that love God, to them who are the called according to his purpose." (A.V.)

"And we know that to them that love God all things work together for good, even to them that are called according to his purpose." (R.V.)

"We know that in everything God works for good with those who love him, who are called according to his purpose." (R.S.V.)

Romans 8:28

This verse gathers up the soft harmonies of a long paragraph which is rich in music: the kind of music which seeks to interpret the mystery of suffering in the experience of God's children. It had begun with a glorious crescendo as it foretold the final and certain triumph of faith: "For I reckon that the sufferings of this present time are not worthy to be compared with the glory which shall be revealed in us" (8:18). But the soaring strain of those words had died away and a deeper chord was struck as he turned to the sufferings of the universe: "We know that the whole creation groaneth and travaileth in pain together until now" (8:22). This was the more subdued tone which accompanied the cry of pain from the ends of the world, and what *we know* in this respect suggests something else which we do not know: "For we know not how to pray as we ought"

(8:26 R.V.). But the sons of God are never without a refrain of comfort: all their adversities are only a prelude to the coming glory. They are comparatively insignificant; they call the power of hope into buoyant activity; they lead to the intervention of the Spirit Himself. The ear of faith can catch the sound of a controlling harmony and the final key is one of lofty triumph: *and we know that all things work together for good to them that love God, to them who are the called according to his purpose.* Those words ring out as the ultimate inference which St. Paul drew from all that he had said about the fact of trial and the triumph of faith. Adversity may be real and profound, but God will bend it for our good: this is the fact which we must grasp with the strength of child-like simplicity, and be content. "God holds the key of all unknown", and faith is glad.[1]

The first part of this verse describes the faith that cleaves to God: *and we know that all things work together for good.* There is much that we do not know, but this *we know* as a fact that admits no doubt: our life is in the hands of God who will guide and control all its issues for His glory. It is only the intuition and understanding of faith which can impart this strong unyielding assurance that *all things* are safe in His hands. Men will sometimes allow that life as a whole is ruled by the will of God, but they shrink from the thought that *all things* have a place in His plan. St. Paul was not afraid to reject the timidity of such reservations and to claim that nothing can take place which does not dovetail with God's purpose for His children. The eye of faith sees that there is room for *all things* in His over-ruling wisdom, and such a phrase should be interpreted in its amplest meaning (cf. 1 Cor. 2:15; Eph. 1:10; Col. 1:20). But the context points with repeated emphasis to the burdens of suffering and affliction (cf. 8:18,38,39). Trial may tempt men to cry out like Jacob: "All these things are

[1] Parker, Hymn 122 in *The Keswick Hymn Book.*

against me" (Gen. 42:36). But this is not how faith reacts nor is it how St. Paul viewed the situation. Our interests are never absent from God's heart; our destinies are never missing from God's hand. It is quite true that we may not always feel that this is the case, but what we feel is not the test of what we know; and faith has taught us that the thread of our lives will never slip between His fingers.

Men are prone to look at things through the eyes of sense and the result is that they think such things clash in hopeless conflict. History is marked by a trail of disaster; providence seems to be void of harmony. Those who are sons of God may be perplexed by trial or numb with pain: they may hardly know what they think; they can only tell what they feel. They are grieved and distressed, and their hearts cry out in anguish: how can this be for good? What good thing can it mean? It is not as though all things are good in themselves; St. Paul did not say that they are. If my child were to die, would that be good? Many things are evil, and evil can never be good. But what St. Paul did say was that God makes all things *work together* for good.[1] He can use all things as means to an end and can adjust circumstances of the greatest adversity and the widest variety to His purpose. He can turn the wrath of man to His praise and can bring the fruit of joy out of the seed of sorrow. We may not know how He brings this to pass; it is beyond human comprehension. But though His will may be mysterious, it is never arbitrary, and we can bow our heads in faith with the knowledge that this inspires.

Therefore faith learns to look away from the lash of pain and sorrow to the good which God has in store. Children who look into the eyes of an earthly father may see the glint of tears in the midst of chastening discipline; and how much more we need to learn that God would not act as He does unless He loved with a love that "never faileth" (1 Cor. 13:8). We need to see

[1] συνεργεῖ.

all things as He sees them if we would know how they work out *for good*. That good is the ultimate fruition of God and of glory (1 Pet. 4:14), for in the words of the Shorter Catechism, "The chief end of man is to glorify God and to enjoy Him for ever". Sometimes men are allowed in this life to see a little of that far-off harvest of good; but in any event they can surely count on doing so in the life to come when all that is now in God's plan will be revealed. Then we shall know how "our light affliction which is but for a moment *worketh* for us",[1] is the direct means of, "a far more exceeding and eternal weight of glory" (2 Cor. 4:17). All the perplexities of providence and suffering which are now so bewildering and so insoluble will then dissolve in the light of His love; sorrow and sighing will vanish away, and the Lord will wipe all tears from our eyes.

The last part of this verse describes the man who cleaves to God: *to them that love God, to them who are the called according to his purpose*. It is imperative not to pause half-way through this verse, because the last words go on to narrow the circle of comfort with a decisive clarity. This makes it clear that the Pauline doctrine that all things are at work for good does not apply to the gay and thoughtless; it is only true in the case of those whose lives answer to the terms which are now laid down. St. Paul began with a comprehensive definition from the human standpoint: *them that love God*. It was with such a text in mind that James Montgomery voiced his noble dictum: "Love God, and thou shalt know."[2] Love is quick to catch the intent of the barest hint where God's will is at work; it has its own instinctive faculty which guides it in its grasp of the secret which words cannot convey. And this is man's experience when the love of God has been shed abroad in a heart that love has made new. Such a man will love Him with a pure and spontaneous love which compels adoration in the words of Simon Peter: "Lord, thou knowest all things; thou knowest that I love thee" (John

---

[1] *κατεργάζεται* op. cit.   [2] Cf. H. C. G. Moule: op. cit., p. 235.

21:17). It is not as though we have read the book of life or heard its roll of names;[1] but "we love him because he first loved us" and gave Himself for us (1 John 4:19).

Those who love God are then further described as those whom God has called. St. Paul began with a subjective description from the human aspect of man's response to God; this was followed by an objective description from the divine aspect of God's summons to man. His phrase aptly defines them as *the called*, and it starts a sequence of strong technical expressions which are well-known terms in Pauline theology. Each term marks a fresh stage in their heavenward pilgrimage, and each is seen from the special angle of God's choice and God's care.[2] St. Paul never spoke of *the called* simply as those who have heard the invitation of the Gospel; he meant those whose hearts have gone out in glad response to the welcome summons of grace (cf. 1:6; 1 Cor. 1:24). It is for God to call; it is for man to come. It is God who invites; it is man who responds. We may respond with the utmost freedom to that divine invitation, but we cannot escape from the fact that it is God who makes the first move. The calling and invitation of God must lie behind the response and obedience of man; His choice always precedes man's choice, whether or not man is conscious of it. Not one link in this chain is forged by man's initiative, or the chain would be so fragile that it would prove worthless.[3] The great doctrine of God's effectual call is meant to teach those who now love God that they must thank Him whom they love. "I ought to have loved God always", so H. C. G. Moule wrote; "it is of His mere mercy that I love Him now."[4]

The call which God addressed to them was in pursuance of *his purpose*. It was not a case of independent freedom of choice:

[1] Cf. H. C. G. Moule: op. cit.
[2] W. Sanday and A. C. Headlam: op. cit., pp. 215–16.
[3] H. C. G. Moule: op. cit., p. 237.
[4] Loc. cit.

it was the plain result of the sovereign intention of God (cf. 9:11; Eph. 1:11; 2 Tim. 1:9). St. Paul set out the two aspects of the human response and the divine initiative alternately and did not draw any exact line of demarcation between the one and the other;[1] but he made it clear that the path which we have so freely followed is a path which had been mapped out in the purpose of God.[2] This means that God always has the end of that path in view, and the great good for which all things now work is part of that purpose and plan. It is stated in terms which lift it far above all the shifting currents of time: it is that we may be fully conformed to the image of His own Son (cf. 8:29). This was St. Paul's inspired definition of the *summum bonum*; it is nothing less than likeness to Christ Himself. And that object will be pursued with a tenacity worthy of God Himself. Nothing therefore can come amiss in our experience when it is shaped in the hand of God to bring His purpose to pass. All the grief and pain of present adversity will fade away as the darkness fades from the hills, for what we know not now we shall know when it is interpreted as part of His purpose.

St. Paul's declaration was made in the spirit of an acknowledged certainty and it furnished a fresh reason why we should look confidently to the future: *and we know that all things work together for good to them that love God, to them who are the called according to his purpose.* St. Paul did not seek to explain the way in which *all things* concur to work out their infallible issues *for good;*[3] but no speculation as to eternal mysteries will bring man's soul so near to God as the humble recognition of this divine purpose.[4] That is why this verse has been a staff for trembling hands and a stay for troubled hearts all down the ages. This was

[1] W. Sanday and A. C. Headlam: op. cit., p. 216.
[2] H. C. G. Moule: op. cit., p. 236.
[3] H. C. G. Moule: op. cit., p. 235.
[4] H. C. G. Moule: *Romans* (The Cambridge Bible), p. 155.

finely illustrated in the experience of John Chrysostom more than fifteen hundred years ago. He was driven out of Constantinople to become an exile in a lonely village in the Taurus mountains where he passed a wretched winter of suffering and privation. At length he was compelled to set out once more on foot with two guards who were chosen for their harsh and callous spirit. It took three months to reach Comana Pontica and the journey was a lingering martyrdom for one whose strength was now worn out. The guards hurried him on without a pause until they were forced to halt for the night at a wayside chapel. He asked again for a further respite in the morning and was driven on for three or four miles until he collapsed with fever. They managed to retrace their steps as far as the chapel, but death was close at hand. John Chrysostom passed peacefully away as he voiced the words of his favourite doxology: "Glory to God for *all things*, Amen."[1] Men who give the glory to God for all things find that all things minister together in God's plan to work out for them a far more exceeding and eternal weight of glory.

[1] R. W. Bush: *St. Chrysostom, His Life and Times*, p. 284.

CHAPTER SEVENTEEN

God's Choice of Man

"For whom he did foreknow, he also did pre-destinate to be conformed to the image of his Son, that he might be the firstborn among many brethren."
(A.V.)

"For whom he foreknew, he also foreordained to be conformed to the image of his Son, that he might be the firstborn among many brethren." (R.V.)

"For those whom he foreknew he also predestined to be conformed to the image of his Son, in order that he might be the firstborn among many brethren."
(R.S.V.)
—Romans 8:29

This verse explains why all things must co-operate for the good of those who love God; it spells out a precise definition of their calling in His purpose: all things must work out for their good because they have been called in the purpose of God, and God's purpose is a settled plan of development which cannot fail. *For whom he did foreknow, he also did predestinate to be conformed to the image of his Son, that he might be the firstborn among many brethren.* This means that the one great good for which all things work is that we may become conformed to the image of Christ, and the supreme purpose in view is that He may be the firstborn in the midst of many brethren. Such words are a commentary on the long and amazing perspective of the love and the care which stretch behind and reach before all God's children.[1] God marked them out in the ages before the world was made and chose them for His own high and special purpose: and this was that in the ages to come they might share the very image of Christ as the Son of His love and dwell as His brethren in the Father's household. This line of thought is based on a doctrine which lies at the heart of Pauline theology: "He hath chosen us in him before the foundation of the world, that we should be holy and without blame before him in love" (Eph. 1:4). The choice of God was the only alternative in St. Paul's view to the idea of just reward for man's merit, and the idea of just reward was one against which his whole mind was in revolt. He went to the limit in order to ensure that no man should have the right to make a demand on God like that of one who would collect his debts: "Pay what thou owest" (Matt. 18:28). He left no room for doubt that the choice of God was an act of grace; it was made long before those whom He chose had been either conceived or born.

St. Paul began with a basic proposition of far-reaching signi-ficance: *for whom he did foreknow, he also did predestinate.* The word *foreknow* with its cognate noun *foreknowledge* is found only four times apart from this verse in the New Testament (Rom. 11:2; I Pet. 1:20; Acts 2:23; I Pet. 1:2),[2] and it always occurs in a context which points to choice either in decision or selection. This was very clear in the case when Peter spoke of Jesus as one who had been "delivered by the determinate counsel and *foreknowledge* of God" (Acts 2:23). It was no less clear when he wrote of those who were "elect according to the *foreknowledge* of God the Father" (I Pet. 1:2). The verb means to take note of, or to fix the mind upon, with a view to making a choice for a special purpose. It is compound in form and the prefix throws the process back from time to eternity; it speaks of that eternal prescience which was necessary for an act of sovereign selection.

[1] W. Sanday and A. C. Headlam: op. cit., p. 214.   [2] προγινώσκω.

This verse makes it clear that it was men and women whom God foreknew with this special kind of knowledge. He took stock of persons rather than of merits, and He foreknew what He would do for them rather than how they would respond to Him.[1]

But to foreknow is not identical with what is meant by the word to *predestinate*; the one must be allowed to precede the other. The word *predestinate* is found only five times apart from this verse in the New Testament (Acts 4:28; Rom. 8:30; 1 Cor. 2:7; Eph. 1:5,11),[2] and it always occurs in a context which rules out the impoverished idea of chance or fate. This was clearly the case when the earliest disciples declared that Gentiles and Hebrews alike had done "whatsoever thy hand and thy counsel *determined before* to be done" (Acts 4:28). It was no less clear when St. Paul declared that "we speak the wisdom of God in a mystery, even the hidden wisdom, which God *ordained* before the world" (1 Cor. 2:7). It means to mark out in advance, to ordain or decree, and it involves a choice for a special purpose. Such deliberate and intelligent choice has nothing in common with a philosophy of fatalism; it is the act of a sovereign volition, and it is in accord with the absolute foreknowledge of God. We may survey a group of things on a table and fix our minds on some rather than on others; thus we know in advance what we will choose and we set them apart with that object in view. And so, whom God foreknew, He chose, He set apart, and this was His sovereign privilege.

St. Paul's next words set out the high purpose which lies behind God's choice: they are *to be conformed to the image of his Son that he might be the firstborn among many brethren*. The word *image* is found in four other verses with a similar reference to Christ (2 Cor. 3:18, 4:4; Col. 1:15, 3:10),[3] and it invites comparison with the special word which is used to speak of

---

[1] H. C. G. Moule: op. cit., p. 156; and *Romans* (The Expositor's Bible), p. 237.   [2] προορίζω.   [3] εἰκών.

H

"the brightness of his glory and the *express image* of his person" (Heb. 1:3).[1] When God made man, it was in His image and after His likeness (Gen. 1:26); but that original image was to become defaced and marred by sin. Therefore when God sent forth His Son as the second Adam, it was once more in His image and after His likeness (Col. 1:15); and His purpose is to restore man in Christ to perfect conformity to that image. This means that we are to reflect His image in our inmost being as the image reflects the original; we are to bear the same moral likeness to Him as He now bears to the Father. He is the Son; we are now sons and heirs who cry with Him Abba, Father. He was "in *the form* of God" (Phil. 2:6);[2] we are to be *conformed* to Him.[3] "We all, with unveiled face reflecting as a mirror the glory of the Lord, are (being) *transformed into the same image* from glory to glory, even as from the Lord the Spirit" (2 Cor. 3:18, R.V.).[4]

This might have been the end in view, but it is not; the great purpose behind the choice of God is that Christ may be seen as *the firstborn* in the midst of many brethren. The word *firstborn* is found in four other verses with a similar reference to Christ (Col. 1:15,18; Heb. 1:6; Rev. 1:5), and it marks His kinship with us while it also preserves His own unique pre-eminence. He is "the firstborn of all creation" (Col. 1:15, R.V.), pre-eminent in time and history; He is also "the first-born from the dead" (Col. 1:18), pre-eminent in might and majesty. He is pre-eminent because He is unique, but His pre-eminence has been heightened because He does not stand alone. The whole purpose of the Incarnation was that He might surround Himself with the many brethren who would do His Father's good will (Matt. 12:48-50). Therefore He Who

---

[1] χαρακτήρ.
[2] ἐν μορφῇ Θεοῦ.
[3] συμμόρφους cf. Charles Hodge: op. cit., p. 283.
[4] τὴν αὐτὴν εἰκόνα μεταμορφούμεθα.

brought the many *sons* to glory is not ashamed to own them as *brethren* (Heb. 2:10,11). He who is the *firstborn* is not alone in the Father's house of many mansions; He has *many brethren* who are fellow members of the divine household. This is the last echo of the theme of sonship in this chapter and it sets Christ as the *firstborn* in the midst of all who are now welcome in the Father's presence as His *brethren*.

St. Paul did not state his teaching about the choice of God merely as an academic issue; his object was immensely practical. The value of theology is seen in an adequate perspective only when its bearing on man's life and conduct has been made plain. Therefore St. Paul's language leaps all hurdles at a single stride in order to guide our thought straight from the choice of God to the glorious destiny of the chosen: *for whom he did fore-know, he also did predestinate to be conformed to the image of his Son, that he might be the firstborn among many brethren.* The great doctrines of grace all have this goal in view; they point to the need for personal holiness, for New Testament sanctity, for true moral likeness to Christ. This is no mere superficial likeness; it is "deep and genuine resemblance due to kindred being".[1] There are some flowers which grow on the glacier's edge, and they are as pale as the snow itself; there are others which grow beneath tropical skies, and they are as rich in colour as the sunlight in which they thrive. This is the way in which virtue reflects and depends on doctrine. The cold climate of a theology which is purely academic will not produce warm and sunny Christian character; but let a man in his inmost being feel the sunshine of the sovereign providence of God and he will stretch every fibre of his spirit to catch more of His grace and to reflect its rays. St. Paul never ceased to marvel at God's choice in his own experience; it was only the grace of God which had renewed him after the image of Christ. And the glorious destiny of which he spoke is well summed up in the words of

[1] H. C. G. Moule: op. cit., p. 238.

St. John: "Beloved, now are we the sons of God, and it doth not yet appear what we shall be: but we know that when he shall appear we shall be like him: for we shall see him as he is" (1 John 3:2).

CHAPTER EIGHTEEN

From Eternity to Eternity

"Moreover whom he did predestinate, them he also called: and whom he called, them he also justified; and whom he justified, them he also glorified."

(A.V.)

"And whom he foreordained, them he also called: and whom he called, them he also justified: and whom he justified, them he also glorified." (R.V.)

"And those whom he predestined he also called; and those whom he called he also justified; and those whom he justified he also glorified." (R.S.V.)

—Romans 8:30

The march of thought in the last verse had passed in one vast swift movement from the fact of God's choice to its final issue; it had travelled from eternity to eternity. This verse returns to trace the steps by which God's plan is put into effect in time and it points to three great landmarks: *moreover whom he did predestinate, them he also called: and whom he called, them he also justified: and whom he justified, them he also glorified.* The idea of sequence in time is a natural concession to the limitations of our mortality. C. S. Lewis[1] pictures time as a long straight line along which we have to journey: we come to each point on that line in turn and we must leave one point before we can move to the next. We stand at a particular point on that line

[1] C. S. Lewis: *Mere Christianity*, pp. 141-5.

at each given moment, and the point where we stand is the present: what lies behind is past, and what stretches before is still future. We are therefore creatures of time who are always looking back or looking forward from a given moment and who see less and less clearly as the distance from the present becomes greater. But God whose throne is in eternity stands quite apart from time: His standpoint in eternity means that He sees the whole time-line from first to last and all at once. There is neither past nor future from that stand-point; all time in that case must be Now. He does not recall yesterday; He does not foresee tomorrow: they are just as clear in His sight as the present moment. He is always aware of the events of time while we see them only as a consecutive series. St. Paul combined both these factors in a context in which time sinks into eternity. His bold sequence of verbs defines each great landmark, and the past tense in each case shows how they appear in the light of glory.

The first landmark serves to fix our minds on the call of God: *moreover whom he did predestinate, them he also called.* The word *moreover* is a particle which is simply rendered by the word *and* in both the Revised and the Revised Standard Versions.[1] Moule calls it the *but* of logic, used here in St. Paul's proof of the security of the children of God.[2] This means that God's call in time is set out as the proper sequel to God's choice in eternity. The four gospels often refer to God's call and God's choice as in contrast, as when Jesus declared that "many are called, but few are chosen" (Matt. 22:14). But such a call may be defined as an outward experience and it is more or less universal in range: "Unto you, O men, I call; and my voice is to the sons of man" (Prov. 8:4). Many may hear that call and yet never respond; and they do not respond because they have not been chosen. But the Pauline letters always present that call

[1] δέ.
[2] H. C. G. Moule: op. cit., p. 238, fn. 3.

and that choice in intimate connection, as when St. Paul argued that "God's purpose of election (must) continue . . . because of His call" (Rom. 9:11 R.S.V.). This is a call which man cannot resist because it is backed by the power of God. He may not want to hear that call, but he cannot help it; he may try to smother its voice, but he does not succeed. It rings with an authority which makes him hear, whether he will or no. And such a call will be effectual; it will move and draw and claim the heart so that he will choose of his own free accord to respond and obey. Thus God's choice of that man issues in a call that leads to his choice of God, and the order is clear: it is for God to call; it is for man to come. "God is faithful, by whom ye were called unto the fellowship of his Son Jesus Christ our Lord" (1 Cor. 1:9).

The next land-mark serves to fix our minds on the work of grace: *and whom he called, them he also justified.* The conjunction is different, but the effect is just the same;[1] the line of thought moves on to show that the result of God's call is that He accepts those who come to Christ as being righteous in Him. God chose them in spite of the fact that He foreknew that they would be in a state of revolt against His law; His call came to them while they were yet in their sin. But He chose them and called them in mercy so that He might receive them for Christ's sake. This means that He acquits them from guilt and accepts them as righteous; He lays their sin on Christ and He lays Christ's merit on them. Thus what was theirs is made over to Him, and what was His is made over to them: and they are "justified freely by his grace through the redemption that is in Christ Jesus" (Rom. 3:24). Luther's statement on this subject was very strong, for his troubled conscience found its only refuge in the substitution of the just one for all who are unjust. "Nos vero debemus involvere Christum," he wrote, "et involutum cognoscere, ut carne et sanguine, ita peccatis, maledictione, morte,

[1] καί.

et omnibus malis nostris . . . Quaecunque peccata Ego, Tu, et
nos omnes fecimus, et in futurum facimus, tam propria sunt
Christi, quam si ea ipse fecisset."¹ This great doctrine lies at
the heart of all Reformation theology and is finely summed up
in the Eleventh Article of the Church of England: "We are
accounted righteous before God only for the merit of our Lord
and Saviour Jesus Christ by faith, and not for our own works
or deservings: wherefore that we are justified by faith only is a
most wholesome doctrine, and very full of comfort."

The third land-mark serves to fix our minds on the fact of
glory: *and whom he justified, them he also glorified.* The particle
which introduced the first statement is now again employed,²
and it ushers in the last step in St. Paul's train of thought. It is
striking to see the way in which he passed direct from the word
justified to the word *glorified* without any mention of the inter-
mediate work of sanctification. This must invite contrast with
the passage in which he spoke of Christ as our wisdom for
"righteousness, and sanctification, and redemption" (1 Cor.
1:30). To be sanctified is the process by which the man who is
in Christ is brought into growing conformity to His image; to
be glorified is the goal of perfect conformity to that image.³
St. Paul did not pause in this verse to speak of the process
because he had the goal in view; he was absorbed in the superb
vision of that final glory. The link between the work of grace
and the hope of glory had already been established: "Therefore
being *justified* by faith, we . . . rejoice in hope of the *glory* of
God" (Rom. 5:1,2). But what was seen in that context as the
hope of glory is seen in this passage as the fact of glory. The use
of verbs in the past tense achieves its most striking effect in this

¹ *D. Martin Luthers Werke, 40 Band, Erste Abteilung* (Weimar, 1911), pp. 434–5.
(Commentary on Gal. 3:13, cf. *In Epistolam S. Pauli ad Galatas Commentarius
ex praelectione D. Martini Lutheri (1531) collectus 1535.*)
² δέ.
³ F. F. Bruce: *The Epistle of Paul to The Romans* (Tyndale Commentaries),
p. 178.

last phrase: *whom he justified, them he also glorified*. The whole process is viewed through the lens of eternity, and the goal is described as it is seen by God Himself. This is comparable with the language in which St. Paul declared that the saints are already seated with Christ in the heavenlies (Eph. 2:6). Thus the glory which shall yet be revealed in us (Rom. 8:18) may be described to our great and endless comfort as a *fait accompli*.

These great doctrines of grace have a dynamic element which will impart moral strength and inspiration to those on whom they may lay hold. So it was in the case of the city of Geneva at a time when Europe was still clouded with the failure of the Reformation in France. It was as when ancient Sparta used to send a single soldier for the encouragement of people in danger. If any corner of Europe had need of a preacher who was willing to face death or torture, a man to be burnt or broken on the wheel, that man was at Geneva, ready and eager to depart, giving thanks to God and singing His praise. And the doctrines which made Geneva heroic in that age of turmoil have an inherent quality which will always confront men with the great question of their personal interest in God's choice and God's call. It is one thing to know that the counsels of God are for ever settled and cannot fail; it is much more to know that men who stand on the time-line can be sure of their part in the plans of eternity. St. Paul was not writing in some impersonal spirit; each word was meant for the strength and consolation of all who are in Christ Jesus. And the Christian assurance which is rooted in firm apprehension of the absolute relevance of such words to one's soul is of supreme value. Augustus Toplady once said that true faith is like a finger, while true Christian assurance is the ring which God loves to place on that finger.[1] The loss of a wedding-ring does not mean that a woman is no longer a wife, but that she will not be content until the ring has been found and is back on her finger. So the

---

[1] Augustus Toplady: op. cit., p. 442.

want of Christian assurance does not make faith less real, but there can be no rest until it is restored. Only let faith lay its finger on these mighty doctrines of grace, and the diamond of full assurance will shine with a special glory.

CHAPTER NINETEEN

If God be For Us

"What shall we then say to these things? If God be for us, who can be against us?" (A.V.)

"What then shall we say to these things? If God is for us, who is against us?" (R.V.)

"What then shall we say to this? If God is for us, who is against us?" (R.S.V.)

—Romans 8:31

One can almost sense a long pause as the splendid words of doctrine came to a close in the last verse. All the varied streams of thought had converged at last in one mighty river, and that river had poured itself out into the ocean of God's final glory. St. Paul had now fully discussed the facts of man's guilt and God's grace, and it may have left him in a mood of adoring reverie. Tertius the scribe would wait until he was ready to speak again; then he broke the silence with a magnificent peroration. The calm voice of reason was now exchanged for the thrilling tones of oratory, and this was in the form of a series of bold rhetorical questions. They were like battle cries which thundered over the field of war, and were in fact meant to show his readers how to use his doctrines in the hour of trial and conflict. Just one challenge might have served the purpose, but he threw out a whole series as if to meet every conceivable situation. Thus he began with the clear and ringing questions. *What shall we then say to these things? If God be for us, who can be against us?* The first question was a favourite formula to sum up what had gone before (cf. 4:1, 6:1,15); here it sums up the whole previous argument. What conclusion shall we draw from these facts? What inference shall we make from such things? He went on at once to reply, but his reply took the form of a further interrogation. If God has set us free from sin and death, given us His Spirit, made us sons and heirs, and chosen us for glory, who can prevail against us? The real effect of this is to reduce all that has gone before to a single mighty statement: God is for us; therefore we have nothing to fear.

The text begins at a distance with words which lay down a condition: *if God be for us.* There were tremendous elements in the very first word: would the congregation in Rome ask *if* God were for them? Many people indeed ignore that *if* altogether and take it for granted that God will be for them. Israel was quite sure that God was for them when they went up against Ai, but they were wrong and they suffered defeat. The Jews were quite sure that God was for them when they disregarded Jeremiah's warnings, but they were wrong and they were forced into exile. The Pharisee was quite sure that God was for him when he gave thanks that he was not like the Publican, but he was wrong and it was the Publican who went down to his house justified. They were all wrong, for God was not for them at all. But St. Paul did not mean to start up the ghosts of doubt and uncertainty in this context. He increased in boldness as he felt the challenge and he seized the very word which might have been used at his expense. The true intent of that word *if* was the very reverse of caution or perplexity; it spoke of a settled conviction and a foregone conclusion. Doubt had melted away in the sunshine of God's declared favour, and the word *if* in these circumstances was the strongest testimony to the fact that God is for us.

This phrase is so remarkable that it compels the mind to go further: would the church in Rome wish to ask how far God would go for them? St. Paul's answer to that question had been furnished with the proofs of His love in the previous argument. God was for us before ever we were for Him; He was for us even when we were against Him. He was for us before the world was made; He was still for us when the world was marred by sin. And the supreme proof that He was for us was the death and resurrection of His dear Son: He was for us when He died on the cross; He was for us when He rose from the grave. This has nothing to do with the necessities of choice on the human level; it is wholly concerned with the realities of grace on the divine level. It is of grace alone that He is now for us in spite of all our sin, and this is the factor which gives St. Paul's words their unique authority. The God who is only found in nature is a God above us; the God who is only known in providence is a God beyond us; the God who is only encountered in law is a God against us: but the God who is in Christ is the God of grace with whom we have to do. "This God is our God for ever and ever" (Ps. 48:14); therefore we may boldly declare that there is no limit to which He will not go for us.

The text ascends to a climax with words which ring out the conclusion: *who can be against us?* There were personal under-tones in the very first word: would the congregation in Rome ask *who* was against them? This would point to something more than hostile circumstances; it could only mean that there were human adversaries in view. Active persecution would create a hostile situation, but the persecutors responsible for it would be direct antagonists. St. Paul was well aware of what this meant; he could speak from his own experience in the city where he was in winter quarters at that moment. The Lord had set before him an open door in Corinth, but there had been "many adversaries" (1 Cor. 16:9). St. Paul had been traduced, maligned, and held up to scorn and contempt: his authority was denied; his integrity was assailed. Such enemies and opponents were against him; but their hostility was not final. He was sustained by the divine promise "I am with thee, and no man shall set on thee to hurt thee" (Acts 18:10). God has never promised freedom from such adversaries; they will always exert themselves to the hurt of His cause and His people. But those who know that God is for them are armed with a strength which will allow them to defy all who are against them.

This phrase is so remarkable that it compels the mind to go further: would the church in Rome wish to ask how far men could go against them? There is no clear line of demarcation to define the limit beyond which such men cannot go; they may pursue the pattern of hostility to the extremes of violence and martyrdom. Adversaries hounded the Son of Man to His death on the cross, Stephen to his death by stoning, James the brother of John to his death by the sword, and Antipas to his death in Pergamos. There were others who were tortured, stoned, sawn asunder, slain with the sword: martyrs whose names are in the Book of Life and of whom the world was not worthy. But no adversary can follow them beyond the point of death: they can go so far, but they can go no farther. It is this fact which gives its force to the searching command: "Fear not them which kill the body, but are not able to kill the soul" (Matt. 10:28). It is even more relevant to the famous saying "Upon this rock I will build my church, and the gates of hell shall not prevail against it" (Matt. 16:18). The gate of a city was the seat of counsel, and the phrase means that the counsels of hell shall not prevail against Christ's church; therefore we may boldly declare that no matter who the adversaries may be, they shall never ultimately prevail.

There is a strong resounding emphasis on the almighty protection which God affords in this ringing challenge: *What shall we then say to these things? If God be for us, who can be against us?* The fact that God is for us means that we should be for God:

the whole relationship should be wholly reciprocal. This is finely illustrated in the case of Martin Luther and his experience at the Diet of Worms.[1] He left Wittenberg believing that it was a summons to death, and he was urged to take refuge a day's journey away from Worms. But he refused to be daunted; he would go on even if there were as many devils in Worms as tiles on the house-tops. On April 16th, 1521, he arrived in the city and made his way through dense crowds to the House of the Knights of St. John where he looked round with his piercing eyes and exclaimed: "Deus erit pro me." He was required to appear before the Diet on each of the next two days, and Thursday, April 18th, marked the crisis when he made his famous speech in reply to all accusations. Luther spoke in Latin, but was asked to repeat it in German. Friends thought that the further effort would prove too much for him, but he went on to add one last word in his own language: "Here I stand." He knew that his conscience was "thirled to the Word of God", and he could do no other. When the Diet adjourned, German friends formed a ring round him while the Spaniards shouted: "To the fire with him, to the fire!" Within a week, he was kidnapped by friends and was carried off to safety in the Castle at Wartburg. It was here that he wrote the hymn so well known in English from its first line: "A mighty stronghold is our God." That hymn was based on his experience at Worms and it reflects the spirit of triumph in St. Paul's cry: *If God be for us, who can be against us?*

[1] T. M. Lindsay: *History of the Reformation*, vol. 1, pp. 273–97.

CHAPTER TWENTY

The Gifts of God

"He that spared not his own Son, but delivered him
up for us all, how shall he not with him also freely give
us all things?" (A.V.)

"He that spared not his own Son, but delivered him
up for us all, how shall he not also with him freely give
us all things?" (R.S.V.)

"He who did not spare his own Son, but gave him
up for us all, will he not also give us all things with
him?" (R.S.V.)

—Romans 8:32

This question is addressed both to the mind and heart with a
combination of logic and appeal which are hard to resist: *he
that spared not his own Son, but delivered him up for us all, how shall
he not with him also freely give us all things?* The logic is rooted in
the facts of history: God did not spare His Son, but gave Him
up for all. The appeal is fashioned with the force of argument:
will God who gave so much withhold what is far less? The
first clause is crowded with elements of emphasis and with
hints of antithesis. It starts with a simple pronoun but that is
not allowed to stand alone; it is solidly underlined by the
enclitic particle with which it is accompanied.[1] The phrase
his own Son points to the infinite difference between the one

---

[1] ὅς γε, cf. H. C. G. Moule: op. cit., p. 239 fn.

who was equal with God, and all others.[1] The Jews had once sought to stone Him because He said "that God was his Father" (John 5:18).[2] He is God's Son in a sense in which we are not: His Sonship is unique, but there is no limit to the number of those who may become sons by adoption. Such traits as these were the ground-swell of St. Paul's thought as he argued his case: this was the claim that the demonstration of God's love which surpassed all else was the gift of His own true Son. This can never be more clearly expressed than in the one famous sentence: "For God so loved the world that he gave his only begotten Son that whosoever believeth in him should not perish, but have everlasting life" (John 3:16). One who loves is always glad to give, and the one who loves most will find most to give. "God so loved . . . that he gave", and in giving, He did not spare even His Son: how then shall He withhold all those lesser gifts which pertain to "life and godliness"? (2 Pet. 1:3).

The first half of this verse directs our thoughts to the supreme act of divine giving: *he that spared not his own Son, but delivered him up for us all.* The word *spared*[3] has overtones and stirs memories which cannot be ignored in a context like this. The same word had been used in the Septuagint when it described the example of sacrifice which beyond all others pointed to that of God who was in Christ "reconciling the world unto himself" (2 Cor. 5:19). This was Abraham's offering of Isaac in obedience to the divine command. God had called him by name and told him what was required: "Take now thy son, thine only son Isaac, whom thou lovest . . . and offer him . . . for a burnt offering" (Gen. 22:2). That quiet lingering emphasis on the one whom he was required to give must have trebled the strain which those words would impose. He had

---

[1] τοῦ ἰδίου υἱοῦ, cf. Rom. 11:24; 14:4.

[2] πατέρα ἴδιον ἔλεγεν τὸν θεόν.

[3] ἐφείσατο.

only one son; he was the child of his old age; yet that was the son he had to offer. That son was the child of promise; in him all the nations of the earth would be blessed; yet that was the son he had to offer. Abraham's willingness to do what God required was a mark of faith and obedience of a supreme order. It won divine recognition in words which haunt the mind: "Thou hast not *withheld* thy son, thine only son, from me" (Gen. 22:12,16). As he spared not his son, his only son, Isaac, whom he loved, so God spared not His Son, His only Son, Jesus, Whom He loved; and what that meant is spelt out by saying that He *delivered him up* for us all. Isaac was rescued by divine intervention, but there was no intervention in the case of God's Son. He was "*delivered* for our offences" (Rom. 4:25; cf. Gal. 1:4): it was *for us,* for our benefit and our salvation that God gave Him up to suffer and die.

St. Paul could not adequately express what he thought of the height and depth of God's love for mankind. God could not love unless He gave, nor could He give less than His Son. This meant that there was sacrifice on the part of God even before there was sacrifice on the part of His Son: God had to give if His Son were to die. This must repudiate all those semi-pagan ideas of an angry God who would not forgive until His wrath had been appeased by the death of the Cross. God could not give His Son except at great cost and with great loss to Himself: there was a sense in which such a gift would impoverish heaven itself because it would be deprived of its chief glory. He did not spare His Son from the trials and infirmities of the Incarnation, nor yet from the pain and anguish of the Passion. He who might have withheld the cup chose to press it into His hands; it was the cup which the Father gave Him whose dregs He had to drain (John 18:11). God could not deliver Him up to die without meeting the ultimate in sacrifice, for there was no other head on which He could lay the sins of all. It pleased the Lord to bruise Him: it was the Father who

put the Son to grief (Is. 53:10). It may be true that what a
man suffers in the person of one whom he loves he will feel
far more than what he is compelled to suffer in himself; it
would cost Abraham far more to lift the knife than it would
cost Isaac to yield. This may suggest that it was more poignant
for the Father to give up the Son of His love than it was for
His Son to die. St. Paul could not think of all that this meant
without breaking into words of awe and worship: "Thanks
be unto God for his unspeakable gift" (2 Cor. 9:15).

The next half of this verse directs our thoughts to the many
other acts of divine giving: *how shall he not with him also freely
give us all things?* This is comparable with the movement of
thought in his treatment of the doctrines of law and grace:
"Received ye the Spirit by the works of the law or by the hear-
ing of faith? . . . Having begun in the Spirit, are ye now made
perfect by the flesh?" (Gal. 3:2,3). St. Paul argued that since
God has done the great thing, He will not leave that which is
less undone: He who accepts us by an act of grace will not
insist on the works of the law as the means to make us holy.
So too this text argues that the transcendent sacrifice which God
made in the gift of His own Son is a sure proof that He will
give all that we need. The Son of Man had laid down the rule
and promise for His servants in their need for food and rai-
ment: "Seek ye first the kingdom of God, and his righteousness, and all these things shall be added unto you" (Matt. 6:33).
God is no man's debtor. He will give far more than we may
ever give up for Him. "There is no man that hath left house,
or brethren, or sisters, or father, or mother, or wife, or children,
or lands, for my sake and the gospel's, but he shall receive an
hundredfold now in this time, houses, and brethren, and
sisters, and mothers, and children, and lands, with persecutions; and in the world to come, eternal life" (Mark 10:29–30).
But this text views the whole situation from the divine stand-
point, and the key lies in the fact that all that God gives, He

gives *with him*: if God gave us His Son, "how shall He not *with him* also freely give us all things?" And St. Paul used the phrase *all things*[1] in its broadest compass: "All things are yours; . . . and ye are Christ's; and Christ is God's" (1 Cor. 3:21–23).

D. M. Baillie made the interesting observation that such words in such a context might be better rendered: "How shall He not with Him also *freely forgive* us all things?"[2] The Greek word not only bears this meaning, but is frequently translated in this manner.[3] This could not be better illustrated than in the verse: "Be ye kind one to another, tender-hearted, *forgiving* one another, even as God for Christ's sake hath *forgiven* you" (Eph. 4:32). It may not be wise to insist on this particular meaning in the case of this text, but it does mark out the ultimate direction of St. Paul's line of thought. God does not give all that we want, but He does give all that we need. St. Paul himself had known what it was to pray for what he wanted and to receive what he needed: he had wanted relief from the thorn in the flesh, whereas what he received was the grace that made him equal to its infirmity (2 Cor. 12:7–9). The effect is heightened in this passage by the use of the words *how* and *also*: St. Paul had laid down his premise, and then, with the help of these words, framed his impressive conclusion as a rhetorical question. This was very like the method he had pursued in an earlier paragraph when he lifted the whole level of thought by the use of the words *much more* (5:10,15,17). We have nothing, but how can He fail to give us all that we need? Needs may be great, but they cannot exceed His grace and love. We will never stand in need of a gift so great as the gift of His Son; then *how* shall He not with His Son *also* give us all things? God might have spared His Son, just as He was

[1] τὰ πάντα.
[2] D. M. Baillie: *God Was in Christ,* p. 178, fn.
[3] χαρίζομαι cf. 2 Cor. 2:7, 10, 12:13; Col. 2:13, 3:13.

willing to spare rebel Israel. But He did not spare Him; He gave Him up. This was love that knows no measure, and what will not that love do for us?

St. Paul often referred to the riches that are stored up with God: there are riches of mercy (Eph. 2:4), riches of grace (Eph. 1:7), riches of glory (Eph. 3:16). This was all summed up in memorable terms when he spoke of "the unsearchable riches of Christ" (Eph. 3:8). The word *unsearchable* suggests something which can never be tracked down to the end, and in this phrase, it hints at wealth beyond all imagination. During the last World War, a jewel merchant found it hard to arrange for the sale of two twenty-five carat rubies which had come into his hands. But he knew that the Nizam of Hyderabad was a man of great wealth and he hoped to persuade him to buy them. A visit was arranged, and the merchant told his story. Then he took the rubies out of an inner pocket and placed them on the table. Nothing was said for a moment— their beauty and lustre spoke for themselves. But the Nizam saw them without surprise, and a servant was sent out to bring back a large steel trunk. This was unlocked in his presence; it was full of little leather bags, each with a ring around its neck. He picked up one, removed the ring, and poured out the contents: some two dozen rubies far more lovely and more precious than the two gems which the merchant had brought. Then he opened another bag and poured out a handful of emeralds; then another which was full of pearls; and so on, until almost every kind of gem lay before his eyes. Nor was this all; when the Nizam spoke at last, it was to tell the merchant that there were still many more trunks in the palace strongroom, all filled with stones like these.[1] This would represent fabulous treasure; yet what is this compared with the unsearchable riches of Christ? And if God has given us His own Son, *how shall he not with him also freely give us all things?*

[1] D. F. Karaka: *Fabulous Mogul* (Nizam VII of Hyderabad), pp. 61-3.

CHAPTER TWENTY-ONE

Who Shall Accuse ?

"Who shall lay any thing to the charge of God's elect? It is God that justifieth." (A.V.)

"Who shall lay anything to the charge of God's elect? Shall God that justifieth?" (R.V.M.)

"Who shall bring any charge against God's elect? It is God who justifies." (R.S.V.)

— Romans 8:33

This series of questions is like the use of a hammer: each stroke drives the nail home with more solid finality. The first question in the series was met by a counter-question: "What shall we then say to these things? If God be for us, who can be against us?" (8:31). This may suggest the real pattern which St. Paul had in mind throughout the whole passage: each clause is a challenge in an interrogative form. This is observed in the case of this text by the reading in the margin of the Revised Version: "Who shall lay anything to the charge of God's elect? Shall God that justifieth? Who is he that shall condemn? Shall Christ Jesus that died?" Such a reading fits the grammar and is "far more congenial to the context";[1] the effect is greatest if there is no interruption in the chain of questions. But dignity and emphasis are not wanting in the traditional reading: *who shall lay any thing to the charge of God's elect? It is God that justifieth.*

[1] H. C. G. Moule: op. cit., p. 240, fn. 1.

St. Paul's language is a distinct echo of the challenge of the divine Servant: "he is near that justifieth me; who will contend with me? Let us stand together: who is mine adversary? . . . Behold, the Lord God will help me; who is he that shall condemn me? (Is. 50:8,9). Doubtless St. Paul had those words in mind as he looked out and defied the world to do its worst. Who shall impeach those who are the elect of God? Shall God who has pronounced them not guilty? The text reverts to the forensic metaphors of the early chapters and the line of thought draws its strength from its very simplicity: no prosecution will succeed if God who is the Judge accounts us as righteous. This is why the question rings out with such triumphant assurance: no one will dare to take up the gauntlet in the court of that Judge.

The first words throw down the challenge: *who shall lay any thing to the charge of God's elect?* The Greek verb[1] is borrowed from the law-courts and is loaded with a technical reference. It meant to bring a charge against a man in a court of justice: he was arraigned; he was accused. St. Paul's challenge would take in all possible accusers, but the Scriptures make it clear that there was one in particular. It is Satan above all who points his finger at the redeemed and shouts *J'accuse!* The Book of Job pictures Satan in his character as the accuser among the sons of God. He brought against Job the accusation of false motives for his integrity: "Doth Job fear God for nought?" (Job 1:9). So too Zechariah saw the high priest in the presence of the angel of the Lord, and Satan standing at his right hand as an adversary to resist and accuse (Zech. 3:1). St. John was yet to hear the loud voice from heaven which would proclaim the true advent of the kingdom of God and the power of His Christ: "For the accuser of our brethren is cast down which accused them before our God day and night" (Rev. 12:10). Satan does not want for material in the work of accusation,

---

[1] ἐγκαλέσει.

and God cannot condone what has been done amiss. Even "the stars are not pure in his sight; how much less man that is a worm?" (Job 25:5,6). Sins which have been done in secret shall be published from the house-top, and no sinner can deny the accusation which they incur. But Job did not defend himself; nor the high priest; nor the brethren: their case was in the hands of God. St. Paul himself would at length be impeached in the presence of the Roman Caesar, but he would lift up his eyes from Nero to the Lord who as "the righteous judge" would resolve the charge (2 Tim. 4:8).

Those who stand at the bar in this context are not outlaws, but *God's elect*; those whom God has chosen as He once chose Israel. They are identical with those whom St. Paul had described in an earlier paragraph: they were foreknown of God, predestinate as sons, called in mercy, and justified, and glorified (8:29,30). The word *elect* always has the ring of sovereign decision: the choice belongs to God; the act is His alone. "Ye have not chosen me, but I have chosen you" (John 15:16). And the safety of *God's elect* is made clear in all kinds of ways. They are the flock of whom the Good Shepherd declared: "I give unto them eternal life, and they shall never perish . . . my Father which gave them me is greater than all, and no man is able to pluck them out of my Father's hand" (John 10:28,29). They are those whom He will raise up and save when they implore His help in the midst of wrong and trouble: "And shall not God avenge his own elect which cry day and night unto him?" (Luke 18:7). And the challenge in this context implies that *God's elect* are safe in His keeping from all accusation. The Son of Man who was unique as God's elect Servant could look His enemies and accusers in the face and could ask: "Which of you convinceth me of sin?" (John 8:46). They could not speak because He was in fact sinless; but it is not like that with us. We are deeply aware that sin has left its stain on heart and life in more ways than we care to think, and each stain may justly expose us to accusation before the bar of God. Conscience may reproach; sinners may deride; Satan may accuse: yet *God's elect* will have nothing to fear, for their case is safe in the hands of God Himself.

The next words ring out in reply: *shall God that justifieth?* (R.V.M.) There is a sense in which the one ultimate accuser is none other than God, for it is God against whom we have sinned: therefore if God does not accuse, no one else can. St. Paul's words point to the day of final judgment and may summon up in our minds the great vision of the seer of Patmos: "I saw a great white throne, and him that sat on it, from whose face the earth and the heaven fled away; and there was found no place for them. And I saw the dead, small and great, stand before God; and the books were opened; and another book was opened, which is the book of life: and the dead were judged out of those things which were written in the books, according to their works" (Rev. 20:11,12). God will be the judge of all hearts when that day comes; nothing will be hidden from His understanding. We know that if we were to say that we have no sin, we would but deceive ourselves; we will never deceive the Lord who knows our hearts and tries our thoughts. Therefore if an accusation were lodged against any of God's elect, they could have nothing to say in reply; they could plead no excuse and would have to confess their guilt. Satan himself is a timid adversary compared with God, and his accusations are of minor account when viewed in the light of divine judgment. We can never sufficiently remind ourselves of the fact that it is the Lord with Whom we have to do. Nero might threaten: Satan might harass; but they would fade into oblivion in the presence of God. St. Paul was so conscious of the greatness of God that he hardly gave a thought to others at all. God is our judge; and as for God, He justifies.

The verb *justifieth* had been the main key-word in the earlier discussion and had been used on no less than thirteen separate occasions.[1] The verb always means *to account righteous,* and now it rings out for the last time in the course of this letter. The great problem of the ages had been summed up by Job in his penetrating question: "How should man be just with God?" (Job 9:2). And St. Paul had faced that problem with the utmost frankness: how can God as our judge be just, and yet pronounce a verdict in favour of the unjust? He had found the solution in the righteousness of Christ which is reckoned as ours through faith. We are "justified freely by his grace through the redemption that is in Christ Jesus" (3:24). It was that redemption which secured His justice and released his mercy; it is the ground on which God can "be just, and the justifier of him which believeth in Jesus" (3:26). It was this great discovery which had transformed Saul the Pharisee into Paul the Apostle, and no doctrine was more basic for his teaching on the forgiveness of sin, acceptance with God, present peace and lasting security. It led him to declare that if men or angels should preach any other gospel, they would be held accursed (Gal. 1:8). If they were to stand at the bar of that Judge with any other plea for righteous judgment, they would undoubtedly face a hostile verdict. This is why the Church in every local situation must stand or fall by this doctrine: it is fundamental to right relationship with God. St. Paul had grasped this fact with a tenacity and an understanding which he never ceased to apply, and its strength and comfort shine through this verse. Who shall accuse the man whom God acquits? Or what accusation will stand when God accounts a man righteous?

It is very interesting to know how a devout Jew whose faith was rooted in Old Testament prophecy might understand the salvation which God had so often promised to His people. Solomon Ibn Gebirol, who was born in Malaga in A.D. 1021,

---

[1] δικαιῶν. Cf. 2:13, 3:4,20,24,26,28,30, 4:2,5, 5:1,9, 8:30 (twice). For cognates, see 1:17, 2:13, 3:8, 26, 4:25, 5:16, 18, 7:12.

wrote a poem called *The Royal Crown*. Two short stanzas are quoted by Abraham in his *Short History of Jewish Literature*:[1]

"From Thee to Thee I fly to win
A place of refuge, and within
Thy shadow from Thy anger hide
Until Thy wrath be turned aside.

"Unto Thy mercy I will cling
Until Thou hearken, pitying;
Nor will I quit my hold of Thee
Until Thy blessing light on me."

That was in the very spirit of the Psalms of David; it adapts their imagery with deep understanding. "Thou art my hiding place" (Ps. 32:7) . . . "I flee unto thee to hide me" (Ps. 143:9). St. Paul might have endorsed that cry; but his experience of grace had brought him to a more absolute certainty. He could never forget how he had once tried to blaspheme the name of Christ and to destroy the Church of God; and yet he had obtained mercy and had found peace with God. He did not stand in his own righteousness, but in the righteousness of Christ, and he knew that God would receive him for Christ's sake. Therefore he could challenge the world without fear of contradiction: *who shall lay any thing to the charge of God's elect? It is God that justifieth.*

[1] Page 64, quoted by John Adams in *The Lenten Psalms*, p. 92.

CHAPTER TWENTY-TWO

Who Shall Condemn?

"Who is he that condemneth? It is Christ that died, yea rather, that is risen again, who is even at the right hand of God, who also maketh intercession for us." (A.V.)

"Who is he that shall condemn? Shall Christ Jesus that died, yea rather, that was raised from the dead, who is at the right hand of God, who also maketh intercession for us?" (R.V.M.).

"Who is to condemn? Is it Christ Jesus, who died, yes, who was raised from the dead, who is at the right hand of God, who indeed intercedes for us?"

(R.S.V.)

— Romans 8:34

It was as though St. Paul could not let this chapter come to a close without one last echo of the mighty proclamation with which he had begun: "There is therefore now no condemnation to them which are in Christ Jesus" (8:1). He caught up that great theme once more in this sweeping question and met it as before in this passage with a counter-question: *Who is he that condemneth? Shall Christ Jesus that died, yea rather, that was raised from the dead, who is at the right hand of God, who also maketh intercession for us?* (R.V.M.). Such a counter-question is more dramatic and more consonant with the spirit of this passage, but the older reading is not without value as a final statement marked by absolute certainty: "It is Christ that died, yea rather, that is risen again, who is even at the right hand of God, who also maketh intercession for us." These words must be read with those of the last verse in order to see how St. Paul placed Christ on the same level with God in the work of judgment.[1] No one can rise up to accuse when it is God who justifies; no one can rise up to condemn when it is Christ who died and rose again: and the ground on which God justifies is "the redemption that is in Christ Jesus" (3:24). This all helps to enlarge our view of what it means to be "in Christ Jesus" and to see why it spells impregnable security. Who will accuse the man who was slain on the Cross? Yet I was there in Him. Who will condemn the man who is at God's right hand? Yet I am there in Him. St. Paul listed four great facts which were like the strands of a mighty hawser. Each was so strong that it could have borne the full strain alone, but their combined strength would result in a massive security. A good literary comparison may be found in the form of an almost credal statement elsewhere: "God was manifest in the flesh, justified in the Spirit, seen of angels, preached unto the Gentiles, believed on in the world, received up into glory" (1 Tim. 3:16).

The first great fact is His death on the Cross: *it is Christ that died*. It is of the highest moment that we should bear in mind the fact that the death of Christ was unique in character and quality. Professor R. G. Tasker has drawn attention to this fact in a fine passage.[2] "There have been many men who have died for others," he wrote; "it is fitting that we should remember them. We may truly say that 'they laid down their lives for their friends'. But great as their sacrifice was, it is surely misleading, and indeed untrue . . . to speak of their deaths . . . as 'lesser Calvaries' or to say 'Christ our Redeemer passed the selfsame way'. For there is only one Calvary; and no one else has

[1] H. C. G. Moule: *Romans* (The Cambridge Bible), p. 159.
[2] R. G. Tasker: *The Narrow Way*, pp. 50-1.

ever trodden or can ever tread the particular self-chosen narrow way that led to it. Only one Man has died for all men, paying the price of sin in its totality, so that His death was their death; and that Man was Jesus of Nazareth. 'I should not mind to die for them', wrote Hilton Young on H.M.S. *Iron Duke* in 1914 as he thought of the Wiltshire Downs and his home at Marlborough:

> 'I should not mind to die for them,
> My own dear Downs, my comrades true;
> But that great Heart of Bethlehem,
> He died for men He never knew.' "

Have we sinned, and do we deserve condemnation? We must confess that it is so. But it is Christ who took our place, and bore our guilt, and died the death that we deserve to die; and God commends His love for us "in that while we were yet sinners, *Christ died* for us" (5:8).

The next great fact is His resurrection on the third day: *yea rather, that is risen again.* Nothing is more remarkable in the apostolic proclamation of the gospel than the constant, basic witness to the Resurrection.[1] St. Paul could not proclaim a Christ that died unless he could also declare that this Christ had risen again. His death removed the ground for our condemnation because He died "for our offences"; but it was His Resurrection which proved that His death was efficacious, and He was "raised again for our justification" (4:25). It is for this reason that the necessary sequel to His death and passion was His Resurrection: this same Jesus who was put to death on the Cross is now alive for evermore. St. Paul used the phrase *yea rather* to show how his argument as to the fact of His death was reinforced by the fact that He rose again. There had been a similar emphasis on a previous occasion: "For if when we were enemies, we were reconciled to God by the death of his

[1] Cf. Acts 1:22, 2:32, 3:15, 4:33, 5:30, etc.

Son, *much more*, being reconciled, we shall be saved by his life" (5:10). St. Paul's phrase *yea rather* does not detract from the atoning qualities of His death on the Cross, but it shows how they were confirmed by the realities of His Resurrection. It was the sign that the debt had been paid and that the bond had been cancelled; it was the proof that there is now nothing more that man must do to atone for sin. It was by the Resurrection that God declared His Son to be "both Lord and Christ" (Acts 2:36). Therefore the man who is "in Christ Jesus" may lift his eyes to the throne of judgment without fear of condemnation, for who is there now to condemn? *Shall Christ Jesus that died, yea rather, that was raised from the dead?* (R.V.M.)

The third great fact is His ascent into heaven: *who is (even)[1] at the right hand of God.* This clause is the only direct statement on the Ascension in the Epistle and it serves to enrich the whole Christology of this passage. The New Testament documents sometimes refer to the exaltation of Christ as though it were one great movement from the grave to the throne, but there was in fact a definite interval of forty days between the Resurrection and the Ascension. These two events were the pivots of His exaltation and must not be confused. The first event declared that He was no longer held bound by death, while the second event made it clear that He shares in the eternity of the Godhead. The real problem of the Ascension narrative lies in another direction. The Ascension from Olivet is a fact which confronts many people with a difficulty even greater than that of the Resurrection: how can we think in terms of a physical translation from some point on the earth's surface to the immediate presence of God beyond all the limits of space and time? But this is to misread the whole record of the Resurrection and to misjudge its real meaning. There is a

---

[1] The word *even* does not belong to the Greek text and should be omitted as in the R.V. and the R.S.V.

THE HOPE OF GLORY

sense in which it may be said that the Resurrection needs the
Ascension as its complement: for how else are we to explain
why He was seen no more of men or what became of His risen
body? And it is plain that a body which could appear or could
vanish at will as a result of the Resurrection was no longer
subject to the laws of nature as in the days of its mortality. We
may therefore justly rely on St. Luke's clear historical account
of His ascent from the Mount of Olives; we may also freely
accept the imagery which describes Him as passing through
the heavens (Heb. 4:14). He has risen from the dead, and in
His risen body, as H. B. Swete declares, "He has passed out of
our present sphere of being into one which is beyond the
furthest limits that we can conceive."[1]

The last great fact is His intercession at God's right hand:
who also maketh intercession for us. He who was once put to death
on the Cross is now alive, ascended, glorified, enthroned, and
has all power and all authority. He is our "advocate with the
Father" (1 John 2:1), and He "ever liveth to make intercession"
for us (Heb. 7:25). Just as before St. Paul had called into use
the phrase "yea rather" to give additional thrust and point to
his thought, so now he used the word *also, indeed* (R.V.),
actually,[2] in order to achieve a like effect. There is tremendous
assurance for us in the knowledge that He is now at God's
right hand; there is greater comfort still in knowing that He is
there as our Mediator with God. St. Paul had already declared
that "the Spirit Himself *maketh intercession* for us with groanings
which cannot be uttered" (8:26–7). Now he employed the
same word to declare that Christ *maketh intercession* for us.[3]
These two forms of intercession are quite distinct and the purpose of each needs to be kept in view. St. Paul referred to the
Spirit as the Author of all realistic intercession in our inmost

[1] H. B. Swete: *The Appearances of Our Lord after The Passion,* p. 106.
[2] H. C. G. Moule: *Romans* (The Expositor's Bible), p. 240.
[3] ἐντυγχάνει.

being, while he spoke of the Son as the mighty intercessor on our behalf at God's right hand. Such language is figurative, for His intercession consists in the fact that He now appears "in the presence of God for us" (Heb. 9:24). St. John was to see him on the throne as a lamb that had been slain (Rev. 5:6): that means that the scars of the Cross are still visible in our advocate with the Father. They are the pleas which He employs, and such pleas the Father will not deny. Therefore the man who is "in Christ Jesus" may lift his eyes to the throne of judgment without fear of condemnation, for who is there now to condemn? *Shall Christ Jesus . . . who is at the right hand of God, who also maketh intercession for us?* (R.V.M.).

St. Paul made one of the greatest affirmations of his apostolic career in a letter to the church at Corinth: "I determined not to know anything among you save Jesus Christ and him crucified" (1 Cor. 2:2). Such a declaration makes it clear that the Cross was the central feature in his testimony to the gospel: "We preach Christ crucified, unto the Jews a stumbling block, and unto the Greeks foolishness: but unto them which are called, both Jews and Greeks, Christ the power of God and the wisdom of God" (1 Cor. 1:23-4). But did this mean that he viewed the Resurrection only as a kind of epilogue to the evangel? Did he fail to regard it as essential to the drama of our redemption? This would seriously misrepresent the whole meaning of St. Paul's great affirmation, for "to know . . . Christ and him crucified" would have no significance at all apart from the Resurrection. The phrase indicates the real direction in which his thought was bound to move, for the proclamation of "Jesus Christ and him crucified" draws all its force from the fact that God raised Him from the dead to die no more. This is why James Stewart declares that to preach "Christ and him crucified" is in fact a Resurrection message, and that we need to recapture its emphasis. "It is one thing to preach the Cross as the last word of divine Revelation. It is quite another thing to preach it as the road travelled once for all by One now known to be alive for ever. This was the stupendous reality which lay behind the onward march of first-century Evangelism."[1] And the meaning of this mighty affirmation is spelt out at length in this verse: *Who is he that condemneth? It is Christ that died, yea rather, that is risen again, who is at the right hand of God, who also maketh intercession for us.*

[1] James Stewart: *A Faith to Proclaim*, p. 111.

CHAPTER TWENTY-THREE

More Than Conquerors

"Who shall separate us from the love of Christ? shall tribulation, or distress, or persecution, or famine, or nakedness, or peril, or sword? As it is written, For Thy sake we are killed all the day long; we are accounted as sheep for the slaughter. Nay, in all these things we are more than conquerors through him that loved us." (A.V.)

"Who shall separate us from the love of Christ? shall tribulation, or anguish, or persecution, or famine, or nakedness, or peril, or sword? Even as it is written, For Thy sake we are killed all the day long; we were accounted as sheep for the slaughter. Nay, in all these things, we are more than conquerors through him that loved us." (R.V.)

"Who shall separate us from the love of Christ? Shall tribulation, or distress, or persecution, or famine, or nakedness, or peril, or sword? As it is written, 'For Thy sake we are being killed all the day long; we are regarded as sheep to be slaughtered.' No, in all these things we are more than conquerors through him who loved us." (R.S.V.)

Romans 8:35-7

This great passage brings the series of questions and counter-questions to a climax with the fifth and the last in the barrage: *Who shall separate us from the love of Christ? Shall tribulation or distress, or persecution, or famine, or nakedness, or peril, or sword?* It was in view of the amazing character of God's known grace that St. Paul climbed to this new and final level of thought. Can anything at all sever us from the love of Christ? Can suffering do what sin cannot do? There is no doubt as to whom he referred: the word *us* has a slight emphasis as a result of its position in the Greek text.[1] Who shall amputate *us,* so loved and so cared for, from the body of Christ? Shall things which we may be called to suffer at the hands of men and demons? It was at this point that he paused to quote the grim words of a Psalm: *as it is written, For thy sake we are killed all the day long; we are accounted as sheep for the slaughter.* This Old Testament quotation forms a parenthesis whose main purpose is to show that there is nothing new or unexpected in the persecution of God's people; and in doing this, it also marks the irrefragable continuity of the Church all down the ages. The series of questions was brought to an end by this apt parenthesis, and the final reply was in words of shining simplicity: *nay, in all these things, we are more than conquerors through him that loved us.* He did not minimise the fact of suffering; he was keenly aware of its effect. He knew that he could not avoid the scars of war; but what of that? His eyes were on the Son of God whose love "never faileth" (1 Cor. 13:8), and whose hand grasps the sword of victory.

St. Paul began with the broadest challenge words could compass: *who shall separate us from the love of Christ?* Such words are in keeping with the bracing vigour and the vivid feeling which mark the whole passage. It was perfectly natural for him to ask *who* when we might have thought that he should have asked *what,* and he chose the word *who* even though he

[1] H. C. G. Moule: *Romans* (The Cambridge Bible), p. 159.

went on to speak of things rather than of persons.[1] This word
in this context is not unlike the words of the gospel about those
to whom the Lord gives eternal life: "They shall never perish,
neither shall *any man*[2] pluck them out of my hand" (John
10:28). The strength of that promise may be gauged by the
great Old Testament promise which was expressly reaffirmed
in the New Testament: "himself hath said, I will in no wise
fail thee, neither will I in any wise forsake thee" (Heb. 13:5,
R.V.; cf. Josh. 1:5). It is true that there are moments when
things, if not persons, may tempt us to think that He has failed
us or that we have been cut off from His love. Such things may
be dark and mysterious, and may almost make us feel that we
now stand where the Son of Man once stood. He was betrayed,
denied, and put to death by men; and that He bore with a
steadfast patience. But when the cloud of sin concealed the face
of God, it was almost beyond bearing. It wrung from His
heart a cry of mingled loss and anguish: "My God, my God,
why hast thou forsaken me?" (Matt. 27:46). That cry was the
measure of a love that has no equal, a love that was stronger
than all the pains of death. That was *the love of Christ* which
this text has in view (cf. 2 Cor. 5:14; Eph. 3:19). Our love for
Him may both falter and fail, but will His love ever fail us or
leave us in the lurch?

St. Paul's counter-question rang out with the valiant defiance
of long experience: *shall tribulation, or distress, or persecution, or
famine, or nakedness, or peril, or sword?* These things rose up in his
mind "like so many angry personalities",[3] and their cumulative
force is almost overwhelming. There are very few who have
had to meet such varied, aggravated, and long sustained forms
of trial as St. Paul (cf. 2 Cor. 11:23–7; 2 Tim. 3:10–12), and
the self-same words weave themselves into the record of many

---

[1] $\tau\iota\varsigma$ not $\tau\iota$. Cf. loc. cit.
[2] $\tau\iota\varsigma$.
[3] H. C. G. Moule: *Romans* (The Expositor's Bible), p. 240.

of his colourful adventures. *Tribulation*[1] referred to the pressure
of some grievous adversity (cf. 2:9, 5:3), such as he had in
mind when he warned his converts: "We must through much
tribulation enter into the kingdom of God" (Acts 14:22). This
was why he gloried in the fact of *tribulation* (Rom. 5:3), and
tried to distinguish it from the agony of what he called *distress*.[2]
The two ideas are in fact quite distinct, and the verbal forms
are used in a way which makes this clear: "We are *troubled* on
every side, yet not *distressed*" (2 Cor. 4:8). Both were closely
linked with *persecution*[3] which had dogged his footsteps ever
since he himself had turned his back on the role of persecutor
(cf. 2 Cor. 12:10). *Famine*[4] refers to the hunger and thirst which
were scarcely avoidable on his journeys. They were joined in
memory more than once with *nakedness*[5] (1 Cor. 4:11; 2 Cor.
11:27). *Peril*[6] was at his heels by land and sea, and at the hands
of Jews and Greeks alike (2 Cor. 11:26), so that he stood *in
jeopardy* every hour (1 Cor. 15:30). And he was at length to
lose his life by the *sword*.[7] Such a list of afflictions was far from
mere rhetoric; it was rooted in the facts of his own personal
history. But what of them? Had they cut him off from the love
of Christ?

This catalogue of sufferings sent his mind back to the cry of
distress which had found vent in the words of a Psalm: *as it
is written, for thy sake we are killed all the day long; we are accounted
as sheep for the slaughter*. The threat from the sword was still
in his mind as he recalled these words, and they are a verbatim
quotation from the Septuagint (Ps. 44:22).[8] It was in that
"song of anguish and faith" that the persecuted remnant of the
Elder Church had poured out their deep lament of suffering
and affliction.[9] It had been for His sake that they were done to
death all the day long; they were "treated like sheep in the

[1] θλῖψις.   [2] στενοχωρία.   [3] διωγμός.
[4] λιμός.   [5] γυμνότης.   [6] κίνδυνος.
[7] μάχαιρα.   [8] Ps. 43:22 in the LXX.   [9] H. C. G. Moule: op. cit., p. 241.

shambles".[1] Nothing could more clearly convey St. Paul's sense of the true ongoing history of God's people than this direct appeal to the experience of an older generation. It is summed up in the moving words of another Epistle: "They were stoned, they were sawn asunder, were tempted, were slain with the sword" (Heb. 11:37). And how did things fare when the Son of Man appeared? He was brought as a lamb to the slaughter, and as a sheep before her shearers is dumb, so He opened not His mouth (Is. 53:7). Such violence and suffering were not confined to Him, for His servants were called to tread the same dark way: for did not one Herod send his henchmen to slay John the Baptist, and did not the other stretch out his hand against James the brother of John? They fell by the sword as others fell by various forms of violence; they were "butchered" like sheep ready for the slaughter.[2] All these things were sober realities; but had they been able to cut the saints off from the love of Christ?

St. Paul's final answer to that question is in words which reverberate with the roll of majestic certainty: *Nay, in all these things we are more than conquerors through him that loved us.* St. Paul had brought forward all the adversities which lie in wait for us, and had recalled how such had been the lot of God's people in all ages. But though crushed or destroyed to all outward seeming, they could soar in spirit above it all. It is the great glory of God's people that they can trust through flood and fire when men who have no faith feel that there is nothing left to live for. The full-throated shout of triumph rang out in that word *nay*,[3] for the very things which threatened to cut them off were the means of "surpassing victory".[4] St. Paul went on to coin one more word of superlative force to express all that was

---

[1] W. Sanday and A. C. Headlam: op. cit., p. 219.
[2] Ibid., p. 219.
[3] ἀλλά but.
[4] W. Sanday and A. C. Headlam: op. cit., p. 219.

in his heart: *we are more than conquerors*.[1] A whole phrase in English is required to translate one strong vivid Greek word and to yield this splendid statement: it was first used in the Geneva Bible and was happily adopted in the Authorised Version.[2] The saints will come through the conflict and will emerge, like the three who were cast into the midst of the burning fiery furnace, with a richer faith and spiritual capacity. And the secret of this thrilling issue lies in the fact that it is *through him that loved us*. The past tense points thought back to His death on the Cross as the crowning proof of a love that will not fail. *In all these things,* we stand on the field of battle; they may inflict pain or sorrow or death: but they cannot cut us off from the love of Christ; it is always steadfast and must prevail.

Those words, written by such a man to the church in such a city, were to come to the proof within a few short years when the converts in Rome were marked for death like sheep for the slaughter. It was not death alone that stared them in the face; there were terrible cruelties as well. Pagan Rome held virginity in such esteem that no woman could be put to death while still a virgin. An edict of Tiberius made such executions impossible; Tacitus, Dio Cassius and Suetonius all bear witness to its results. The first case in point comes from a pagan household: Tacitus recorded the facts, but they are too sad to repeat. The records and legends of those who were put to death for Christ's sake disclose how this law was enforced in the persecutions of the first three centuries. This means that the maiden who is listed as a Virgin Martyr had gone to the place of execution as one who was little more than any other despised slave prostitute in the eyes of the vast majority in that pagan city. They knew that her virginity had been destroyed; her soiled garments, reeking from the lupanar, told the story of her defilement.[3] Had this cut her off from the love of Christ? Was

---

[1] ὑπερνικῶμεν.　　　[2] W. Sanday and A. C. Headlam: op. cit., p. 222.
[3] Cf. Hugh Northcote: *Christianity and Sex* (second edition, 1916), pp. 349 ff.

she left in the lurch? *Nay, nay, nay!* What they did not know was that God looked upon her as "the king's daughter" who is "all glorious within" (Ps. 45:13). But St. Paul's words apply to the ordinary humdrum levels of life no less than to those fields of high heroic suffering. There may be times when the humble heart is tempted to feel that God has forgotten to be gracious. But what can pluck us out of His hand or cut us off from His love? Can disappointment? or sorrow? or difficulty? or weakness? or loneliness? or trouble? or pain? *Nay, in all these things we are more than conquerors through him that loved us.*

CHAPTER TWENTY-FOUR

No Separation

"For I am persuaded, that neither death, nor life,
nor angels, nor principalities, nor powers, nor things
present, nor things to come, nor height, nor depth,
nor any other creature, shall be able to separate us from
the love of God, which is in Christ Jesus our Lord."
(A.V.)

"For I am persuaded, that neither death, nor life,
nor angels, nor principalities, nor things present, nor
things to come, nor powers, nor height, nor depth,
nor any other creature, shall be able to separate us from
the love of God which is in Christ Jesus our Lord."
(R.V.)

"For I am sure that neither death, nor life, nor
angels, nor principalities, nor things present, nor
things to come, nor powers, nor height, nor depth,
nor anything else in all creation, will be able to separate us from the love of God in Christ Jesus our Lord."
(R.S.V.)
—Romans 8:38–9

The great barrage of questions and counter-questions had burst
in swift staccato succession. It had begun like the roar of
distant thunder as he looked out on the field of battle: "What
shall we then say to these things? If God be for us, who can be
against us?" (8:31). And it swelled in strength and volume as

the climax was reached: "Who shall separate us from the love of Christ? Shall tribulation, or distress, or persecution or famine, or nakedness, or peril, or sword?" (8:35). The air was tense, but his voice was full of triumph as he gave his final reply: "Nay, in all these things we are more than conquerors through him that loved us" (8:37). We might have thought that with such words, Tertius would lay down his pen and St. Paul would fall into silence. What more was there to say? Had he not now lifted his eyes, and ours, to the highest summit that faith can scale? Such a sentence would have been an adequate conclusion for this moving peroration; further words might only spoil the effect. But St. Paul did not stop just there; he had still more to add. Sin cannot cut us off from Christ, for it is Christ who died to save us from our sin; sufferings cannot separate us from His love, for His love for us was manifest by His sufferings. Therefore St. Paul caught up the last question and his voice passed into direct statement with the final glorious crescendo: *For I am persuaded that neither death, nor life, nor angels, nor principalities, nor powers, nor things present, nor things to come, nor height, nor depth, nor any other creature, shall be able to separate us from the love of God which is in Christ Jesus our Lord.*

St. Paul's typical expression, *for*,[1] had been used fifteen times in the course of this chapter and now appears for the last time: *for I am persuaded.*[2] His clear sense of logic was felt once more as he spoke for himself and it ushered in a verb which has the resonant qualities of strong personal conviction. This may invite comparison with the former saying: "For I reckon" (8:18). That was a term of bold calculation; this is a term which speaks of a well-grounded assurance (cf. 14:14, 15:14). His mind was free from the haunting shadows of doubt; he was utterly persuaded that God would hold him fast. Three years later, he stood in chains before Agrippa and made his great self-defence. It rose to a climax with a direct appeal to the king

[1] γὰρ.   [2] πέπεισμαι

to declare his faith in the prophets, but the king brushed it off with a vague and enigmatic reply: "Almost thou *persuadest* me to be a Christian" (Acts 26:28).[1] St. Paul's comment on the miserable uncertainty of that reply revealed his own amazing confidence: "I would to God, that not only thou, but also all that hear me this day, were both almost, and altogether such as I am, except these bonds" (Acts 26:29). He was thoroughly persuaded; nothing could shake that strong rock-like belief. Nor did he change his mind when he wrote his final letter, knowing that death by the sword was at hand: "For I know whom I have believed and *am persuaded* that he is able to keep that which I have committed unto him against that day" (2 Tim. 1:12).[2] He knew all the threats and hazards of the future, but he was not dismayed; he was wholly convinced that the love of God would carry him through.

St. Paul at once went on to list the kind of things with which we must contend but which will not prevail: *neither death, nor life, nor angels, nor principalities, nor powers, nor things present, nor things to come, nor height, nor depth, nor any other creature.* It was quite in keeping with his style to personify abstractions, but it is not easy to tell how far each of them was meant to express a new idea.[3] All but two of his terms are in couplets, and the grouping of ideas in couplets has a subtle appeal. The first couplet was that of *death* and *life*: he had nothing to fear from the loneliness of the one nor from the afflictions of the other. Then he referred to those malign forces which are active in the unseen world of spirits: the *angels* and *principalities*, invisible, mysterious, against which we have to wrestle in a ceaseless conflict (cf. Eph. 1:21, 3:10, 6:12; Col. 1:16, 2:15). The word *powers* stands next in the Authorised Version, and Moule thought that "rhythm and the affinity of words" both point to this as the correct order in the sequence of terms (cf. 1 Cor.

[1] πείθεις.   [2] πέπεισμαι.
[3] Cf. W. Sanday and A. C. Headlam: op. cit., p. 224.

15:24; Eph. 1:21, etc.).[1] But the overwhelming authority of the manuscript evidence is in favour of the subsequent position which the Revised Version adopts: "perhaps . . . in the rush of impassioned thought," he would insert the words just as they came.[2] It was a wide term which took in all those forms of being in the spirit world which might prove hostile to Christ and His servants. Then he referred to *things present* and *things to come*, words which sum up all the measureless dimensions of time, and to *height* and *depth*, which sum up all the limitless proportions of space. Height and depth were terms of astrology, and point to the stars which were thought to affect human destinies.[3] Then in one last sweeping phrase, he declared that there was nothing *in all creation* (R.S.V.) which can sever us from the love of God.

St. Paul's train of thought runs out in the final statement that none of these things *shall be able to separate us from the love of God which is in Christ Jesus our Lord*. It is impossible to avoid a comparison between the two lists of things which seem to threaten separation. The first is a comprehensive list of perils in the material world to which we belong, and it comes to a head with the threat of death from the sword (8:35). And the second is a no less comprehensive list of perils in the unseen world of spiritual forces with which we must contend, and it starts with the fact of death as the other ends with that of the sword (8:38,39). St. Paul dared to claim that none of these things, whether alone or in massed and hostile array, can cut us off from God. He was firmly convinced, that "neither the crisis of death nor the calamities of life",[4] no hierarchy of spirits, nothing in time or in eternity, no invisible powers, nothing in heaven or on earth, nor anything else in all creation, can come

---

[1] H. C. G. Moule: op. cit., p. 241, fn. 2.
[2] W. Sanday and A. C. Headlam: op. cit., p. 223.
[3] A. M. Hunter: op. cit., p. 87.
[4] J. R. W. Stott: op. cit., p. 127.

between us and the love of God. Separation from the presence of God is the last and the most dreaded evil that man can face, but St. Paul had no fears. The pronoun now reverts to the plural and there is a decided emphasis on the word *us*. It can only refer to those who are *in Christ Jesus* (cf. 8:1); those who are in living union with Him. They are members of the body of which He is the head, and they are as necessary to Him as He to them. There will be no mutilation of that body, for none of its members will be cut off. The words of Christ Himself are the bed-rock on which this claim must rest: "My Father which gave them me is greater than all, and no man is able to pluck them out of my Father's hand" (John 10:29).

The last phrase in this text serves to expand and to define St. Paul's earlier reference to "the love of Christ" (8:35) through the use of a deeply interesting equivalent: *the love of God which is in Christ Jesus our Lord*. The love of Christ may be isolated in a way that helps to focus our minds upon the Son of God as one whose love "passeth knowledge" (Eph. 3:19). But that love is only described in full when it is shown as a demonstration of God's love for the world (John 3:16). The love of God had poured itself out in the love of Christ, and that love was stronger than death itself. This is why there is such endless music in St. Paul's phrase: *the love of God which is in Christ Jesus our Lord*. Such a definition was a fitting end for this great chapter; it leads thought right up to that name at which every knee is to bow. That name had in fact rung like a peal at the end of the last four chapters; it was as though St. Paul meant to sound its cadence at the close of each stage of his unfolding argument. Imputed righteousness is a reality which is meant for us all "if we believe on him that raised up Jesus our Lord from the dead" (4:24). The grace of God will reign through such imputed righteousness "unto eternal life through Jesus Christ our Lord" (5:21, R.V.). The gift of God is in contrast with the wages of sin, for it is "eternal life in Christ

Jesus our Lord" (6:23, R.V.). And the hope of deliverance from the thraldom of sin is "through Jesus Christ our Lord" (7:25). This name breaks like a wave on the shore of human understanding with each successive argument until at last in this verse it is heard once more like the voice of many waters with the sound of final triumph.

St. Paul wrote those words while in the house of Gaius who was his host during a winter at Corinth. Neither St. Paul nor the Church in Rome could have then foreseen how short a time was to elapse before they would stand in need of all their comfort. St. Paul himself would be put to death by the sword not far from Rome at Tre Fontane, and his readers were the men and women whose blood was to soak the sands of the great Roman amphitheatres. Nero would come to the end of his reign in a storm of appalling cruelty and those who bore the name of Christ would be tempted by a terrible dilemma. They could save their lives if they would deny His name; they would lose their lives if they should confess their faith. But the honour of Christ was safe in their keeping and they did not fear to die as martyrs for Him. Some were mauled to death by wild beasts; some were slain by the sword. Many were soaked in pitch and tar before they were fastened to poles in the palace gardens: they were living torches who lit up the darkness of the night as they burned in shirts of flame. What then? Had God left them in that hour of horror? Had they been cut off from the love of Christ? No; in all the agonies of such martyrdom, they were invincible. And when they fought their last fight with beasts and demons, perhaps they drew strength and comfort from those great words. For they were so sure that nothing could come between them and the love of God: not death, nor life; not Nero, nor Satan: for they were safe in the clasp of that love which is in Christ Jesus our Lord.

Postscript

Robert Bruce (1554–1631), the disciple of John Knox and Andrew Melville, died at Kinnaird on July 27th, 1631. He had come to breakfast and his younger daughter sat by his side.

"As he mused in silence, suddenly he cried: 'Hold, daughter, hold; my Master calleth me.' He asked that the Bible should be brought, but his sight failed him and he could not read. 'Cast me up the eighth of Romans,' cried he, and he repeated much of the latter portion of this Scripture till he came to the last two verses: 'I am persuaded that neither death, nor life, nor angels, nor principalities, nor powers, nor things present, nor things to come, nor height, nor depth, nor any other creature, shall be able to separate us from the love of God which is in Christ Jesus our Lord.' 'Set my finger on these words,' said the blind, dying man; 'God be with you, my children. I have breakfasted with you, and shall sup with my Lord Jesus this night. I die believing in these words.'"

–D. C. MacNicol: *Master Robert Bruce* (1907), pp. 270–1